Behind the
Gold Curtain

I wish to acknowledge my appreciation to Annick Cohen, Marian Landew, Margo Slade, and Eleanor Berger for their valuable assistance and encouragement in the preparation of this book. — D.S.

Photos courtesy of Metropolitan Opera Archives, Metropolitan Opera Press Department, and Local 802, A.F. of M.

780.92
Berkowitz

Behind the Gold Curtain

Fifty Years in the Metropolitan Opera Orchestra

~~~~~~~~~~~~~~~~

DAVID BERKOWITZ

in collaboration with
DOLORES SOYER

BIRCH BROOK PRESS

Copyright © 1995 by Dolores Berkowitz Soyer

All rights reserved. Except for brief excerpts in reviews, no part of this book may be reproduced in any form or by any means without written permission from the author and publisher.

First edition.
Library of Congress Catalog Card Number: 95-076145
ISBN: 0-913559-29-6 (hardcover)
ISBN: 0-913559-30-X (paperback)

Published in the United States by

Birch Brook Press
P.O. Box 81
Delhi, NY 13753

Write or call for free catalog of books & printed art.
In NYC, (212) 353-3326.

Composition by
Pro•To•Type
Middletown, NY

Printing by
Royal Fireworks Press
Unionville, NY

Hardcover binding by
Spectrum Bindery
Florida, NY

To all my colleagues, who encouraged me to write the story of the Metropolitan Opera Orchestra from our perspective as players.

Contents

Introduction i
Metropolitan Audition 1
The Early Years 5
Conductors, Musicians, Performers 15
Orchestra Life 27
Singers 33
More About Conductors 43
Rehearsals & Orchestra Procedure 47
The Merchant Marine Years 53
The Metropolitan Opera Orchestra After World War II 59
Labor Relations at the Met 77
Stalemate at the Opera 83
Orchestra Personalities 95
The Met on Tour 109
The Touring is Ended — A Long Summer Ahead 121
The Changing of the Guard 127
The Bing Era 137
Epilogue 167
Illustrations .... center

Introduction

It all began when I was eight years old and won a Hershey bar after my first violin lesson. I continued to win one each week, thus satisfying my taste for sweets and my parents' wishes for me to have a musical education.

My first teacher, who taught woodworking in the small town of Warren, Ohio, where I lived, also taught violin as a hobby to a group of eight students. My first violin was rented from my school for $5. It was made in Japan of compressed molded wood, and bore a Stradivarius label.

Not surprisingly, the instrument did not have much sound. Still, what sound I produced prompted my mother to look for a more professional violin teacher via the local conservatory, the Dana Musical Institute.

A Miss Eatwell was the answer, at least until two years later when my family moved to Long Island, New York. My mother made certain the violin came with us. The school agreed to sell it to us for an additional $5.

For the first few months in New York, I neglected the violin while adjusting to a new school, a new neighborhood and no teacher. The last was remedied by a piano salesman, who was soliciting door to door. My mother told him we had no use for a piano — not yet — but we were looking for a capable violin teacher. The salesman said he knew just the man, a qualified musician who began his career in Italy and continued his studies at Yale and Columbia. His name was Demo Caruso.

Instead of calling for an appointment, he arrived at our home a few Saturdays later about 7 PM in the midst of a blustery snowstorm. We were having a children's party that evening. My mother was shocked to see a man covered with snow from the brim of his fedora to his soaking spats, and a walrus-shaped mustache dripping melted snow from his face.

She could not very well turn him away into the storm, so she invited him to our party. He soon asked if another room was available so that he could give me an audition. I played. He said I had some talent, and should continue to study. I began to study with Mr. Caruso immediately, and soon became convinced he was an excellent teacher and musician.

My worst enemy was my inadequate violin, which Mr. Caruso constantly criticized. A new one was needed, but the lack of money was a problem. Fate intervened when I broke a neighbor's window while playing ball on the first day of my summer vacation.

My mother promptly told me that I must find a job to pay for the window now and a new violin later. I set out frantically, covering an area of about three miles, going from store to store. At the end of the day, I found one man who was willing to hire me because of my dexterity in handling tools. I was to repair bicycles for $10 a week. During the eighth week of my employment I suffered a hand injury and saw fit to end my job, rest up for the approaching school term, and begin looking for a better violin.

A friend of our family was in the pawn brokerage business and he referred me to an art dealer who imported art, furniture, antiques, and as a hobby, he collected violins for his personal use. After listening to me play, he brought out one of his favorite violins and sold it to me for $75. I was then about twelve years old. Some forty years later I sold this instrument for $1,200.

When I entered Richmond Hill High School I joined its orchestra and became concertmaster, and had the good fortune to meet Morton Gould. He had appeared as piano soloist during one of our assembly sessions. We soon became close friends until he left during his second term to accept a music scholarship at New York University. To continue our friendship, and so that he might learn to conduct, I suggested we form a small orchestra.

We were able to obtain every instrument except a viola; indeed, no violist was available anywhere. The lack of a viola was critical. Morton was at the piano conducting with one hand and playing the missing parts with the other. I told him that conductors are supposed to use both hands. He replied, "I can't because we don't have a viola."

I suggested to Morton that I could borrow one from my high school and try to solve its mysteries. Morton taught me how to read the alto or viola clef, just as the pianist must learn the bass as well as the treble clef. This was the beginning of my career as a violist.

I studied alone for two years. Then the head of the music department, Mr. Woods, recommended that I try out for the New York Philharmonic Scholarship. At age sixteen, I applied and won the audition for Queens and Brooklyn. This New York Philharmonic Scholarship was granted to talented high school students who then studied with the first chairs of the New

Introduction

York Philharmonic Orchestra. My teacher was Rene Pollain, who was the assistant conductor of the New York Symphony under Walter Demrosch. Pollain later became the first violist of the New York Philharmonic and assistant conductor to Arturo Toscanini.

It was under Mr. Pollain's guidance, patience, and inspiration, that I began to understand the difference between the violin and the viola. We studied harmony, theory, composition, and orchestration with Winthrop Sargeant, a former member of the New York Philharmonic, who later gained fame as the music critic of the *New Yorker* magazine.

It was during this period in the early 30's that I became interested in chamber music. As a violist I was in greater demand than a violinist or cellist. I received more invitations and opportunities to play with various groups than I could handle and this gave me the greatest experience, knowledge, and confidence that I could possibly get in such a short space of time.

It was then that I was invited by Samuel Weiss and his brother, Henry, to join a new string quartet sponsored by the New York Philharmonic, where they were both scholarship students. Another student, a cellist, Nicholas Tonhazy, also joined us. The group was coached by Imre Pogany, principal of the second violins, and a former member of the famed original Budapest String Quartet. All repertoire was played from memory.

Our progress and success was almost instantaneous, and as our popularity spread, more performances became available. We adopted the name, New York Philharmonic Scholarship Quartet.

Radio station WQXR (then W2XR) invited us to become their first official quartet in 1934-35, and we changed our name to the Oxford String Quartet. We were to perform every Sunday evening during prime time, 7 to 8 PM. Our broadcasts were the first radio broadcasts of chamber music in the United States. Eddy Brown, the Musical Director of station WQXR, suggested we add a soloist each week, such as a piano, flute, or clarinet to perform a more varied repertoire and give WQXR more prestige by having known soloists.

We agreed, eventually inviting a flutist named Milton Wittgenstein. He never left, and our quartet became a chamber group, the Oxford Ensemble.

Wittgenstein's influence with the management in selecting soloists and repertoire caused us to lose interest in this type of programming as a string quartet, and as we were also making changes in personnel in our quartet, we ended our affiliation with station WQXR.

Our first violinist left to join the St. Louis Symphony, and was replaced by his brother, Henry Weiss. A new second violinist, Harold Kohon was engaged. I was also engaged by the Metropolitan Opera, so our days as a quartet were numbered; we disbanded.

All during this period, I still continued my academic studies, attending St. John's Law School until 1934, when I realized that my future was in music. I thought it advisable to audition for the National Orchestral Association, the most important training orchestra for young professional musicians, headed by Musical Director, Leon Barzin. He was formerly with the New York Philharmonic Orchestra. Upon being accepted, I ended my legal aspirations, and gave my full attention to music, much to my mother's dismay.

My two years of playing with the National Orchestral Association constituted the best professional experience I might have gained anywhere in the country. It prepared me for my first audition and the beginning of a new career.

— David Berkowitz

Metropolitan Audition

My audition for the Metropolitan Opera orchestra in 1936 is etched in my mind forever. Approximately a third of the orchestra was being replaced or re-auditioned, although I was not aware of this at the time. The management wished to replace the older members, and generally upgrade the orchestra. One of our quartet members heard about the audition on Friday afternoon. It was to be held the next day — Saturday morning. We called the Metropolitan immediately and were invited to audition the next morning at 10 AM.

It was all very primitive. The audition was conducted on the roof stage of the old Metropolitan Opera House. It was built to hold one hundred people, but some two hundred applicants squeezed in.

We were separated from the conductors by a curtain so they could hear but not see us. The man conducting the audition was the Personnel Manager and first trombonist of the orchestra, Simone Mantia. His method was to choose people at random, point and say, "You. You play next." The noise and confusion was nerve racking; it was impossible to concentrate. After waiting around for four hours, I told the manager that I did not see any hope of playing my best and winning a place. I did not even know how many openings were available, and some of the violists I heard auditioning impressed me as being far more experienced than I. I told Mr. Mantia that I wanted to leave. He said, "You! You play next."

At 2:30 PM my opportunity arrived. I was given fifteen minutes of sight-reading — consisting of Wagner, Strauss, Verdi and Mozart, the most difficult and unfamiliar music in the repertoire. I was also given a choice of solos. The entire audition lasted less than half an hour.

Today the audition system is entirely different. The applicant must send in a resume and a tape. If you are selected for the audition, the music is mailed to you for study at least a month in advance. That way the performer can be well prepared and avoid the traumatic experience I and so many others endured.

After my audition, I was very discouraged and expected nothing. Within a month, however, I received a call from Mr. Mantia asking if I would be interested in a Metropolitan Opera contract. Naturally, I jumped at the opportunity. I was told that I would be notified when rehearsals would begin prior to the season's opening in the fall. I was so young and inexperienced that I did not understand the meaning of the orchestral contract. I thought you were engaged to play until the management wished to dispense with your services.

My excitement was so great, I forgot to ask about the salary, working conditions, or any other requirements spelled out in the contract. We were still in the Great Depression. I could see that this contract, whatever its terms, would give me the financial stability I required for my parents and myself.

The salary was $128 a week, which covered eight performances a week minimum (seven nights and a Saturday matinee). Rehearsals were paid at $2 an hour. We rehearsed almost daily, and sometimes on Sunday mornings. Our time was spent performing, rehearsing and traveling back and forth to the opera house — four trips daily, six days a week. The season was short in those days, and during the season we had no time to be with our families. Nobody complained very much, however, least of all myself.

When I joined the orchestra many changes were taking place. Most of the musicians were foreigners who spoke English poorly or not at all. The rest were Americans. Music was the only common language, and even then miscommunications plagued us. This was also true of the conductors. They spoke only their native tongues, and we had difficulty understanding them.

The foreigners were a mix of Italians, Germans, French, a few Russians, Hungarians, and Swiss. They had greater operatic experience, but we were catching up rapidly. The new openings were being filled by young Americans. Most of them had excellent training from the Juilliard School, The Curtis Institute of Music or colleges such as Oberlin. In addition, the finest music teachers were settling in or visiting the United States.

The result was a great deal of resentment and jealousy on the part of the older men in the orchestra. They chided us and made fun of us. Their interests were different from ours: We wanted to demonstrate our virtuosity so that we could hold on to our jobs, while they had proven themselves long before. Whenever we had a break, they discussed politics, family life and such, while we reviewed difficult passages.

BEHIND THE GOLD CURTAIN

When I joined the Metropolitan Opera in 1936 a new management had replaced the Gatti-Casazza regime. Herbert Witherspoon was the new general director but never lived to start the season. He was replaced by his assistant, Edward Johnson, a former tenor with the Metropolitan Opera. Edward Zeigler continued as assistant general manager and Earl Lewis continued as head of the box office and subscriptions. A staff of assistants, including the financial, clerical and telephone operators was maintained. The rest consisted of personnel to operate the physical end of the opera house such as maintenance, ushers, libretto sales and ticket takers.

The biggest problem facing management was financial, especially how to combat the Depression. Sacrifices had to be made in every department.

The stage suffered the most because of torn and worn scenery, the absence of new productions and a reduced staff of directors. Herbert Sachse was in charge of the German operas, while Herbert Graf and Desiree De Frere shared the balance of the repertoire, with an occasional guest director invited for a new production. To save money, the stage rehearsals were kept to a minimum of time for the artists and chorus — a standard considered unacceptable today.

I recall De Frere's style in trying to save the company money by leading the chorus from one end of the stage to the other, filling in empty spaces so mob scenes would look realistic. He constantly reminded Edward Johnson of how much money he was saving the company by not hiring extras and by cutting down rehearsal time. Compared to today's Hollywood standards in opera, it was amazing that the stage directors were able to mount twenty operas during a season in a fourteen or fifteen week period.

Let me give a more thorough picture of the orchestra's financial structure for that period. Our contract called for eight performances a week at $128, plus additional pay for rehearsals and extra performances, which brought our average weekly wage to approximately $200. The season then consisted of about seventeen weeks including two preliminary weeks of rehearsals, a three week tour for some and, occasionally, extra performances. The rest of the year we were free to seek other musical engagements, teach, or do nothing. By these calculations, the average opera musician could realize about $4,000 annual income from the Metropolitan Opera alone.

Compare this to other professions in the New York area during the 1936 period: School teachers, civil service employees, firefighters and police officers were averaging $35 a week or about $1,800 annually. Not surprisingly, I felt far more fortunate than the average, earning more than twice as much, and being free from financial worries for a while. Those musicians who returned to their homes and families in Europe were able to live in even greater style because of the greater dollar value.

The manner in which we were paid then would bring laughter and criticism from today's musicians. On Fridays we would walk up a flight of stairs and into a tiny cubby-hole of an office filled with boxes of records piled high. Our paymaster was Amy Gerber, fulfilling one of his many tasks.

Those were the days before withholding tax, social security, and a number of other taxes that appear in today's statements. After we signed, he would hand us an envelope with cash. At the end of the year we were given a slip of paper with the necessary information needed for income tax purposes. Taxes were so low by today's standards, we were able to keep most of our earnings.

But those were also the days before any sort of benefits were available to musicians or any other members of the opera company. Civil service employees, school teachers, workers in large corporations were beginning to receive medical insurance, pensions, unemployment and social security benefits. In our case, if we did not work we did not get paid. Vacation was unheard of. We had many weeks of unemployment when we could enjoy our free time, but at our own expense. Fortunately, some of the younger members could foresee the problems we might have to face.

As a result, we took matters into our own hands. Our members inaugurated a sick benefit plan amongst ourselves on a contributory basis. Each member paid $10 weekly to build up this fund so that a sick member would receive $50 each week whenever he was ill or for the balance of the season up to one year.

Our formal uniforms consisted of tails, white tuxedo shirt, white vest and tie. For matinees we wore striped pants, cutaway jacket or a dark suit. We paid for them all, even instrument insurance. In future negotiations with management, however, these expenses and improved benefits became part of our contracts.

The Early Years

Backstage at the Metropolitan Opera House were the musician's quarters and dressing rooms, replete with antiquated steel lockers — difficult to lock and full of plaster and dust from the crumbling ceiling. This is where we stored our instruments and tuxedos. The passageway under the stage that some musicians were required to cross to get to the other side of the pit resembled a dungeon filled with old props, junk and cobwebs.

There was also an elongated table about three by six feet, set in the center of the room. All our business was conducted at that table. All our instrument cases were left there, too, since the orchestra pit was already too crowded. When the performance ended everyone was in a hurry to leave for home, but it required another few minutes to find your case in and among the pile.

In the pit, the chairs were made of bentwood with wicker seats that bore the indentations of many years of rear ends. Some of the seats were torn and so uncomfortable, especially in view of the many hours we spent sitting on them, that many of us developed back trouble. The first question of the day was always, "How is your back today?"

We tried to make ourselves comfortable in various ways: Some musicians used pillows tied to their chairs, even inflated medical cushions (whoopee cushions). I wore a motorcycle belt tightened to the last notch. It impeded my circulation, but it helped me get through the day.

To add to our difficulties, many of the scores and music parts were in shambles, torn and covered with candle wax from before the days of electricity. I especially remember the music parts from the "Flying Dutchman," "Rienzi," "Samson and Delilah" and a few other scores that looked as if they had been soaked in a tub of water.

The rehearsal hall was on the fifth floor of the opera house. It was a dismal place, doubtless left uncleaned since the opening of the house in 1883, almost fifty years before. The windows were partly black; dust covered everything and there was just enough light coming in to prove that there were windows. We could barely see the back of the room, which was crowded with scenery and props, and other theatrical paraphernalia. The opera house, it seems, was expanding and had growing pains. There was no room to store antiquated scenery and costumes, so every corner had junk in it.

We had very short breaks at rehearsals (only five minutes of every hour of rehearsal compared to fifteen or twenty minutes of each hour of rehearsal today) and we used these breaks to stand and stretch and wander the room. Some, very few, practiced the passages they did not know. One group would congregate at these dirty windows, fascinated with whatever they were seeing.

The windows faced Seventh Avenue, the middle of the garment district. There were factories and showrooms on the east side of the street, and we were on the west side. The building extended between 39th and 40th on Seventh Avenue. If you stretched your neck, you could see down almost to 38th Street.

There was always a view of some showroom where a model was displaying furs, gowns, even underwear and negligees to buyers. All we cared about was the models. We did not see them undressing, but we did see them very skimpily dressed at times, and of course, we all had vivid imaginations. We had this wonderful view constantly, until the windows became blacker and blacker and all you could see was a faint light coming through, so this diversion came to an end.

We had two antiquated elevators backstage that looked like cages. The one on the stage door side at 39th Street was in a little better condition. It worked more consistently. The other was on the 40th Street side and was strictly a local. Still, musicians generally used the elevator on the 40th Street side.

It took at least five minutes to ride non-stop to the fifth and top floor; nonstop trips were a rarity. Generally, the elevator stopped at each floor to allow someone to get out with costumes or props. The wig department was on the second floor, and the costumes were stored in large wardrobes on each floor. If you arrived five or ten minutes prior to a rehearsal, you could be sure that those minutes would be absorbed going upstairs, and you would surely be late.

Many younger members walked up the five flights, but once you got to the top, to get to the rehearsal room you had to walk over the stage via the "flies" (a walkway). It was just like walking the plank. This walkway was made of some thick metal, and every sound from each step resounded as if you were inside a tunnel. It also swayed from side to side; you prayed that you'd make it.

If you did not live in Manhattan and did not have time enough to go home between rehearsals and performances, you had to stay in the city from the first note of the rehearsal to the last note of the performance.

No luxurious air-conditioned dressing rooms for us; no real limit to the number of rehearsal and performance hours either. Intermissions were comparatively short, so there was little time to rest and relax.

There were no nights off, unless a Mozart, Cimarosa or light opera was scheduled. Then there might be one or two performers let off for the evening. My first night off was spent attending a Cimarosa opera. Some of our first stand performers (these were section leaders) had an agreement with management whereby they were off one night a week, and for some of the woodwind and brass players, more often.

Prior to my joining the Met, many of the musicians and chorus returned to their homes in Europe at the end of the short seasons. A few owned villas dating back to the time of Caesar, Charlemagne and King Charles. Their families remained in Europe all year. To save expenses, the chorus would be transported back and forth each year from Europe as a boatload, since they were the best trained chorus available, and able to sing in the languages of the opera.

One violinist returned to his villa in Belgium each spring with a trunk load of soiled laundry. He had it washed and cleaned there in one day at a fraction of the cost in New York. He would wear paper dickeys instead of tuxedo shirts and then dispose of them at the end of the week. This all started to change prior to World War II as the musicians and singers became American citizens and settled in the United States.

Our eating habits and arrangements were not much better than our working conditions, giving credence to the idea that all musicians have bad stomachs. There were no set times for dinner or lunch during those early years. We grabbed a bite whenever there was a break during a rehearsal or performance. I would often have to combine lunch and dinner during the late afternoon, and travel to the opera house during the normal dinner hour. The meal I enjoyed most was usually at 1 AM after the performance.

The Metropolitan Opera made a practice of keeping the house dark on some Tuesdays each month. On those days we traveled to Philadelphia, and occasionally to Brooklyn and Newark. Many of us enjoyed this change because the time was spent traveling in a private train assigned to our company, and the leisurely dinner we were able to enjoy was different from our usual rushed dining. However, the discomfort of a strange theater, such as the Academy of Music in Philadelphia, made it difficult to perform. With their cramped orchestra pits and even smaller stages, these theaters were not built for opera performances.

The trip home was a nightmare. It was a milk-train that promised to get you home for breakfast, but you never knew what time that would be. Nevertheless, we were expected at the 10 AM rehearsal, alert, with a new conductor either trying to charm us with his genius, or trying to thrust his lack of genius down our throats. We eventually dropped Philadelphia because of the increasing cost of transporting the opera company back and forth for one performance. Our final appearances in that city were tacked on to one of our tours and lasted for an entire week.

Baltimore was also included in short out-of-town tours. These tours took place during the last week of the New York season. The week was split, half in Baltimore, the other half in New York. This was all prior to the long annual tour.

The company looked forward to these long tours. Our routine was much easier than during the New York season. Rehearsals ended before the tour, so the need to travel home and back was eliminated. You just walked a short distance from your hotel to the theater. Our eating habits became more relaxed and normal. It was almost like a vacation with pay, except for the separation from one's family.

The annual tour traditionally began in Boston, which was recognized as the second most important cultural city in the east after New York. Boston, one of our oldest American cities, had much to see and visit. It was my first opportunity to explore the New England coast and many inland points of interest, including many fine restaurants. We particularly enjoyed the Boston Opera House which was built in the European tradition and had wonderful acoustics.

Some of my older colleagues did not look forward to touring. Many were foreign and could not find the type of food they enjoyed, so they prepared their own in their hotel rooms. Some spent the mornings shopping. One older gentleman in particular from Newark was an excellent chef. He would come on tour with enough food for the first five days, stashing it outside his window sill, which acted as a refrigerator.

He carried pots, pans, and an alcohol burner, the result of which was a first-class feast. On one occasion after a long opera, when all the restaurants were closed, I was invited along with Izzy Blank, our first trumpet player, to dine. The menu was a feast of veal rollatini, pasta and rum cake, and

Italian wine to wash it down.

Our next stop was usually Cleveland, Ohio. We were in the downtown business district. The area was deserted by 5:30 in the evening; only a few hotels and restaurants were open and available to our large traveling company of about three hundred. Worse, to enjoy the public attractions and see the residential areas one had to travel through very large industrial sections that seemed devastated because of the Depression in the mid-30's.

The auditorium was a huge public arena built for conventions and sporting events without any concern for acoustics. It seated ten thousand or more people. The topic of conversation between patrons sitting in the rear with those sitting up front included questions of who was really singing, and how did they sound? The poor acoustics and great distances from the stage hampered the performance immensely.

Not surprisingly, Atlanta, our next stop, was a refreshing change. Although Atlanta was the financial center of the southeast, it was beginning to develop in the field of art and music. Since the era of Caruso in the 1920's, Atlanta's ambition was to have the Metropolitan Opera visit each spring. And we did, in the middle of the blossoming magnolia season. The city, as always, welcomed us with open arms and southern hospitality.

The theater where we first performed was an old boxing arena that had the odor of a gymnasium. Every night the hall filled with a beautiful audience in full dress and flowing furs. The next season they moved the performances to their Fox Theater, a beautiful hall that comfortably seated five thousand. A civic center was built in the mid-70's and is the present home for entertainment in Atlanta.

None of the theaters on our tours had the facilities of the Metropolitan, but our company always made the most of the situation. New sets of scenery were made in New York to fit the smaller stages. Space in the pit was much less, so we had to squeeze as many men as possible into the pit, or use a smaller compliment of strings. No matter, the audience and critics usually loved every opera we offered them.

After the war, during the 1948 and '49 seasons, the opera extended these tours over eight or nine weeks and across the United States. Eventually they were discontinued, mainly because of artistic and financial considerations, and the objections of the personnel being away from New York for this length of time. Eventually our tours returned to a six or seven week period, which included a week split among Memphis and Dallas, Houston, San Antonio, Minneapolis, Chicago, and one week divided among Toronto, Montreal and Detroit. Then home.

These cities were chosen because they represented the best cross-section of the mid-west to the east, and because of their interest and support for opera. The cities also guaranteed the costs. What surprised me most about these out-of-town audiences was the knowledge of opera they had acquired mainly through our weekly radio broadcasts.

Our methods of travel changed radically during my fifty years with the Metropolitan Opera. Our company of approximately three hundred people, comprising stagehands, carpenters, electricians, tailors, dressmakers, make-up artists, financial staff, orchestra, chorus, ballet, conductors, artists (singers), and management staff, were all part of these tours. We used two sets of Pullman trains, twenty cars — traveling a few hours apart to each destination. The technical staff and chorus left first; then the artists, management, orchestra, and music staff (conductors and pianists/coaches) followed. These Pullman trains were antiquated and usually used for the transportation of groups such as circuses or baseball teams. There were many mechanical failures and no air conditioning. Besides, we had to wait many hours for seating in the dining cars.

The more modern railroad equipment was reserved for commercial travelers. Traveling in these trains was unforgettable.

The younger members were usually assigned an upper berth above the wheels of the train, and each connection of the rails was felt with a thump. Even though these tours were a change from our New York routine, as they grew longer and longer, the wear and tear began to show. In the early fifties our traveling conditions began to improve when each member of the company was given a private roomette in a modern air-conditioned train. A few cities such as San Antonio, Oklahoma City, Des Moines, and Rochester, engaged the opera for one performance so the roomette served as our hotel, affording us a bit more comfort.

About 1967 we began to travel by air when Eastern air offered the Metropolitan Opera chartered plane service. This move enhanced Eastern's prestige as well as changing the overall picture of our future tours. Now three to four hours became the maximum time necessary to travel from one city to another. We were able to stay in a hotel each night and return home for a day in case of a family emergency. The scenery, costumes, musical instruments and the like were shipped to our next destination after each performance.

The most important attraction of these tours were the stars who were known through recordings, radio, and concert appearances. These artists welcomed the opportunity to sing opera, and to improve their popularity for future solo engagements in many of the smaller cities throughout the United States. Community and civic concerts were just beginning to organize and were attracting top musical stars at guaranteed fees. Our nation was offering golden opportunities to talented stars via radio and the new medium, television. The star singers, therefore, were most willing to travel on the tours, enhancing their careers and bringing enjoyment to the public.

Some stars became opera legends: Flagstad, Melchior, Rethberg, Thorberg, Schor, List, Kullman, Varnay, Traubel, and others who sang mostly German operas, which in turn became more popular at the Metropolitan during the 1930's. As a result, some of the more popular Italian repertoire was being replaced. The eight or nine performances in each city on tour usually listed three German operas.

The Italian and French operas we brought on our tour were performed by the great artists of the era who sang on the Metropolitan stage in New York. A few of these included Pons, Ponselle, Grace Moore, Rise Stevens, Albanese, Sayao, Pinza, Martinelli, Martini, Thomas, Crooks, Baccaloni, Maison, Tibbett, and others. Most of our performances were sold out in advance with some auditoriums, such as Cleveland, St. Louis and Toronto, seating more than ten thousand people.

I recall a Friday evening in 1938 in New Orleans when we were to perform "Rigoletto." An announcement was made that Lily Pons, Lawrence Tibbett, and Norman Cordon were indisposed and would have to cancel. There was an immediate uproar in the audience; people demanded a refund. The following day a Saturday mantinee of "Hansel and Gretel" was scheduled for a youthful audience. Because of the previous evening's fiasco, only two hundred people showed up. That performance was canceled and the money, refunded, It was the first and last time in my experience that a performance was canceled because there were more people in the cast than in the audience.

In my second season, I was a great deal more relaxed. I knew the routine of the house and I had much more confidence in myself. I felt I had proven my competence as a violist and had won the respect of colleagues.

There were many changes in the viola section after the first year. Dmitri Mitroupoulos became the music director of the Minneapolis Symphony, and chose David Dawson to be his first violist. Giuseppe Fick was a friend of John Barbirolli, and when Barbirolli became musical director of the New York Philharmonic he took Fick with him as a violist. Nathan Gordon left to join the NBC Symphony under Arturo Toscanini.

I was advanced to the second stand. My partner was Gabriel Peyre, the oldest and longest serving member of the orchestra at that time. He had joined some years before the San Francisco earthquake, and it is said he loaned a pair of trousers to Enrico Caruso when the tenor lost his clothing in the earthquake. (The Metropolitan Opera was on tour at the time.)

Mr. Peyre had been in the orchestra for at least thirty years in 1936. He was experienced and of considerable help to me. He always warned me about tricky spots in the scores, but to such a degree that I became overanxious; in a sense, his cautionary advice did me more harm than good. Instead of playing with freedom and abandon, I was tense and nervously anticipated every rough spot in the score.

In my first year it was all work and no play. The endless practicing of the opera repertoire, the travel back and forth from Long Island where I lived created enormous pressure. I was always worried about the train schedule and had to sprint to the opera house from Pennsylvania Station to make the curtain on time.

The second year I spent more of my time in the city after rehearsals. A number of us, all commuters, would play ping pong or go to the 42nd Street library. We did everything we could to enjoy the few hours before the evening performance.

On Saturday nights, if we were scheduled for a Sunday morning rehearsal, instead of going home after a performance, we went to the Turkish baths at the Luxor Hotel to spend the night. There were about eight of us. We played cards, used the equipment at the baths and steamrooms, and on Sunday morning arrived promptly for the rehearsal and in good condition.

In the season of 1937-38 we prepared an opera by an American composer, Richard Hageman, who was then one of the prominent Hollywood composers. The opera was called "Caponsacchi." It only lasted one season and then left the repertoire. A new opera required extensive rehearsal, and we had to do this on extra time, usually on Sunday morning, and occasionally on Saturday morning before the matinee performance.

There had been other American operas introduced at the Metropolitan, "The Emperor Jones" by Louis Greunberg, for example, "Through the Looking Glass" and "Peter Ibbetson" by Deems Taylor. Unfortunately, I never had the opportunity to play them as they were introduced in the early 30's, before I joined the company; they were dropped from the repertoire, usually after one season.

I imagine the main reason was that during the Depression years, the management could not afford to spend the extra money. New repertoire requires a lot of rehearsal. The company was familiar with the standard repertoire, which meant fewer rehearsals and thus less money spent.

The procedure at the Metropolitan for introducing new repertoire is the same. Standard operas are eliminated and others are added. Repertoire is created or changed for a particular singer, or to introduce a new one — like Zinka Milanov.

I recall her debut in 1937-38. She was heralded as a young, sensational soprano from Yugoslavia. Her debut at the Met was in the role of "Leonora" in "Il Trovatore" by Giuseppe Verdi. I remember the commotion at the time. The management had never seen her and when she arrived they found her "slightly" overweight — more than twice the size they had expected. The costume department, accustomed to camouflaging very large people, found itself with a problem it could not handle. The management insisted she lose some weight. She did, and since her voice was truly extraordinary she went on to become one of the greatest Metropolitan Opera stars, the queen of the dramatic soprano repertoire.

Another debut that season was that of the great Swedish tenor, Jussi Bjoerling. He had produced many records and had a built-in following when he came to the Met. The management needed tenors to replace the great tenors of the 1920's. Caruso was gone and Benjamino Gigli had left because of tax difficulties with the U.S. Government. So Bjoerling was a welcome tenor, and a very valuable addition to the roster. (Gigli did come back later in 1938-39 for five performances, including "Lucia di Lammermoor," "Traviata," and "Tosca," after someone with power on the Board of Trustees arranged tax concessions for him.)

Bjoerling made his debut in "La Boheme" and was sensational. In those years he sang mostly lyric roles and later included some of the more dramatic operas of Verdi and Puccini in his repertoire.

Conductors, Musicians, Performers

Conductors are supposed to be vital to the success or failure of a good opera performance. An opera company like the Metropolitan usually carried six to ten regular conductors and as many as ten or twelve assistants on its staff, necessary to handle its extensive repertoire in the various languages.

Early in my career at the Met, conductors were in complete charge, and had the authority to hire or fire a musician for practically any reason. They were also assuming greater importance in the interpretation of musical scores.

The old practice was for a conductor to start an orchestra off with a down beat, permitting them to play their best and occasionally guiding them to the end of the music with a prayer that the orchestra would end together.

Many conductors also tried to cast a spell over the audience with fancy gestures and movements that they felt enhanced their prestige, but this only tended to confuse the orchestra more and accomplished nothing. There are a few conductors who deserve the recognition as great musicians and interpreters, but not many.

Primarily it is the job of a conductor to direct an opera performance with inspiration, coordination, knowledge and expertise. This is easier said than done, for most conductors may be lacking one or more of these qualities. To be able to coordinate a team in the hundreds — chorus, ballet, supers, stage hands, orchestra and soloists — can be a monumental task. It is like a ball game where the results cannot be determined until the very end. Because of these great responsibilities, few successful conductors have achieved great prominence in the operatic field.

A very important role in an opera company is that of assistant conductor. The assistant conductors are usually pianists, staff conductors or coaches.

Their duties are varied. They teach singers new opera roles, and accompany singers in the orchestra pit when the orchestra is not available for stage rehearsals. In the early years the conductors were sent to the apartments of the stars to rehearse them and coach them to convey the musical ideas of the conductor in charge of their performances.

The assistant conductors cued in the chorus and stage bands, from the wings, if a direct view of the conductor in the pit was not possible. In the old house before closed circuit TV the assistant conductor would cut a hole in the scenery, stand on a ladder and relay the conductor's beat to the performers on stage. There are a number of operas that call for either on-stage orchestra or band, and sometimes off-stage orchestra and chorus.

For instance, in the last act of "La Traviata," sounds of music and singing are heard through the open window. In "Don Giovanni" at the end of the first act there is an orchestra on-stage and in the last act, last scene there is also an orchestra on-stage. They cannot see the pit conductor because there are stage drops in front of them so the assistant conductor is backstage to cue them in at the proper time. There are many instances when the people on-stage cannot see the pit conductor because of the action and it is the backstage conductor's job to convey the main beat to those people.

Often the assistant conductor is in the orchestra pit, just behind the conductor taking notes. Sometimes the conductor wants to hear what the balance was like, and he walks to the rear of the auditorium to see if we, the orchestra, were covering the singers, and if certain choirs of the orchestra were well balanced. In these cases the most competent of the stage conductors took over the pit conducting until the conductor returned to the pit and relieved him.

In many instances when we played with backstage conductors, we were surprised at how competent they were, and we applauded them. Artur Bodanzky would use his favorite phrase, "Good Boy!" and pat them on the back. Of course, if the assistant was too good, a second opportunity never came.

When I started my career with the Metropolitan Opera orchestra in 1936, the most important conductor was Artur Bodanzky who made his reputation in Europe as a Wagnerian conductor. He was hired by the Metropolitan Opera in 1915. His importance and reputation in the U.S. began to grow with the expansion of the German repertoire. By the 1930's he became our leading conductor, with sufficient authority to help select the musical staff for the Italian, French and other repertoire.

I found him to be very strict, stern and a tough taskmaster. Often during a performance he would glance in the direction of the younger men with threatening looks and gestures that were frightening to the entire orchestra. If he heard a wrong note or noticed incorrect bowing from the strings, he would glance in that direction continuously and try to intimidate the suspected player with his gestures and shaking his fists. There were many stories about his authority that we feared, because he had the power to make decisions at the end of the season — who was to remain and who was to be dismissed.

Bodanzky usually kept his head buried in the score while conducting, occasionally glancing around the orchestra to see if he had everyone's attention. If he noticed a musician yawning, blowing his nose, turning a page or perhaps resting, he immediately became suspicious and focused his attention on that musician.

The viola section had five new members, John DiJanni, Nat Gordon, David Dawson, Frank Clawson and me, so we received a great deal of attention when Maestro Bodanzky conducted. It was during a performance of "Tristan and Isolde" during the orchestral prelude that the viola section has a tutti solo passage ascending chromatically. Bodanzky expected us to bow the passage of six notes separately instead of one bow or legato, as it was written. When he looked in our direction to cue the violas in this spot, he noticed one musician bowing up instead of down.

He immediately began to gesticulate with his left hand at the entire viola section and continued to glare at us for most of the act. We all felt in jeopardy not knowing who might be the guilty player and suffer the penalty.

At the end of the act he exited in our direction and stopped to speak with the entire viola section. The entire orchestra's eyes were focused on us, anxious to watch the outcome. He addressed us calmly, simply saying, "Gentlemen, in this particular passage, I implore you, especially you younger men, please use longer separate bowing so that in the future it will sound more emphatic."

We were greatly relieved, naturally, to hear him address us as a group instead of any one individual. Generally, he would focus his attention on one person in the woodwind or brass section if he was guilty of playing a wrong note. He would curse that person under his breath for the entire act. The older men knew the repertoire and felt more secure, but the younger men sometimes lived in terror.

We had two very capable Italian conductors who shared the Italian and French operas. Gennario Papi was one of the most capable conductors, born to opera, that I have ever encountered. He was a will-o-the-wisp, about four and a half feet tall, under one hundred pounds, poor eye sight but full of energy. A protégé of Toscanini, he was engaged by the Metropolitan Opera in the early 20's. He conducted everything from memory, which was a very unusual feat among opera conductors. Unlike a symphonic conductor, an opera conductor must be able to cue the singers, chorus, ballet, orchestra and anyone else connected with the performance. It made everything much easier for the entire cast to know that the conductor had everything under control and in the palm of his hand or baton. If he wanted to emphasize a dynamic he would jump up and down on the podium to draw our attention. To attract a musician for a cue he would look in his direction and make a sound with his lips, like calling a cat.

In the last act of "Carmen," when the reoccurrence of the famous theme from the "Toreador" aria begins, Papi tried to warn the flutist directly in front of him of his approaching solo by using his pussy-cat whistle. The flutist was day-dreaming and joined the orchestra late, much to the anger of the conductor. When the act ended they both settled the issue with an explanation from our flutist, Arthur Laura, who had a sense of humor of his own. He simply told Maestro Papi, "When you make that sound with your lips I do not think of a cue, I think of a cat."

Many conductors are paranoid about the personnel they deal with every day. They consider it a personal affront if a musician steps out of line or makes a mistake. My first unpleasant experience with Maestro Papi occurred during a performance of "Pagliacci" and "Cavalleria Rusticana," or "Ham and Eggs" as it is called. I happened to be sitting at the last stand near the exit from the pit. We usually perform "Cavalleria Rusticana" first and "Pagliacci" second.

When the librarian collected the music after the first opera, he mistakenly took the part for "Pagliacci" from the stand and left "Cavalleria Rusticana" behind. When we returned after the intermission to play the second half, I noticed the "Pagliacci" part was missing. I whispered to my partner that I would run up to the library for the correct opera during the prologue of "Pagliacci" and I returned within a few minutes with the correct part. Maestro Papi saw me leave and return to the pit. This immediately aroused his curiosity and his suspicious nature. He sent for me after the opera, and I thought I would be fired on the spot, without any explanation, for leaving the pit. When I told him the facts, I do not think he believed my story, as he did not understand much English, and he never believed musicians anyway, but he did not reprimand me.

The opera repertoire was very new to me as compared to the symphonic literature. My first season the operas seemed to arrive fast and furiously. Before I had time to learn an opera it was on to the next. I spent hours at home practicing, trying to learn one opera after another. The season

BEHIND THE GOLD CURTAIN

consisted of twelve weeks, in which we performed as many as eighteen to twenty operas, whereas today in an annual season of thirty weeks we perform only twenty to twenty-four operas.

Obviously, the opportunity to repeat an opera eight or ten times a year, compared to three or four times in 1936, offers a decided advantage to a musician today. No sooner had I gotten my fingers into an opera like "Lohengrin" or "Othello" and the next opera would be performed. Each opera has its tricks, traps, and difficulties, and it takes years to learn them. Repeating an opera more frequently in the performance season offers a great advantage in absorbing not only the technical difficulties but the composer's intentions. The Puccini operas were the most tricky and difficult for me in the beginning, because of his style, but with a few years experience, the operas became so natural to me I was able to play most of my music from memory.

Conductors and orchestras face each other like generals and their armies in battle. The responsibilities of the Metropolitan Opera conductors were to inspire, enchant or tame the performance and orchestra to the public's and critic's delight. If they failed they could be dismissed.

Unlike armies, which see the field of battle, musicians can spend a lifetime never once seeing the action on stage. The orchestra is too busy playing and has too poor a view to be able to watch. It was during a performance of "La Boheme," with Maestro Papi conducting, that I decided to take a look as the first act was ending. I stood up to see Mimi and Rodolfo exiting off stage, and Maestro Papi turned to the viola section with a tremendous accented beat to emphasize the action on the stage. Everybody played — except me. Papi immediately sent for me after the act and I expected the worst.

He shook his tiny fist at me and exclaimed in broken English, "Ehh, whatta happen there? Why you no play?"

I looked at him, trembling, without a legitimate answer. He knew I was watching the stage, which was considered a cardinal sin for a new member. I got off lightly this time with just a reprimand. Still, over the years, I became a habitual stage watcher; I just didn't get caught.

The other conductor who shared the Italian and French repertoire was Ettore Panizza who began his career in Italy and settled in Buenos Aires as head of the Teatro Colon. He was able to divide his conducting time between both continents because their winter is our summer.

Panizza was a very capable and knowledgeable conductor who knew the standard repertoire thoroughly. He spoke no English. As a result, all of his interpretation and authority came from his baton and hands. The orchestra as a whole greatly appreciated his professionalism and enjoyed working with him.

The last permanent conductor was Wilfred Pelletier, a friend of and accompanist for Edward Johnson, our new manager, who rewarded him with this opportunity. He was a fine musician, coach, and rehearsal pianist, but lacked conducting experience. He gained it on the job. He would bury his head in the score, hands raised above his shoulders, and follow the singers until something would go wrong during the performance. He would suddenly look up in the direction of the mishap but too late to correct the situation and then lose his place in the score. The musicians finally had an opportunity to relax a bit, free from constant observance and fear.

Pelletier's assignment was to conduct the popular Sunday night concerts, which were a conglomeration of famous opera arias featuring the less important singers. The results were a mishmash that the audience thoroughly enjoyed.

The comprimarios or supporting singers and the promising young artists were given an opportunity to display their abilities during these Sunday night concerts. Each artist selected an aria from his or her favorite opera and sang it impromptu without an orchestra rehearsal. This was the librarian's big job for the week, for he had to distribute fifteen to twenty opera parts to each stand in the orchestra. A book mark was placed in each part where the aria was to begin and after the applause for each singer we would scramble for the next opera part, ready to accompany the next singer.

These were the days before photocopying, which could have saved everyone a great deal of effort and energy. Occasionally, one of the popular radio stars or prima donnas would appear for good measure, such as John Charles Thomas, Richard Crooks, Lily Pons or Rise Stevens.

We all enjoyed these performances because it gave us an opportunity to hear arias from operas that were seldom performed and new to many of the younger musicians. And there were always mishaps in which one or more orchestra members would get lost and struggle to end with the singer. Nobody seemed to know the difference, least of all our conductor, Wilfred Pelletier.

The audience loved every minute of these performances. Some twenty years later I had the occasion to perform with Maestro Pelletier in Puerto Rico where it was obvious he had gained a great deal more confidence and knowledge, able to interpret and lead the orchestra and cast through a good performance.

It was during this period that Maestro Bodanzky's health began to fail; he was seldom able to finish a performance. He would assign one of the younger conductors to complete the opera, usually Carl Reidel, who was a fine musician and knew most of the operas by memory. His main problem was that he lacked a good conducting technique and seemed timid, hardly the qualities recommended to become a successful conductor.

One of the Metropolitan's fortunate acquisitions was Erich Leinsdorf, who fled Europe and Hitler to join our conducting staff as an assistant. Legend has it that Leinsdorf walked to Salzburg from Vienna to apply for a job with the opera. He soon became affiliated with Bruno Walter and Arturo Toscanini, following which he was recommended for a position at the Metropolitan for the 1937-38 season.

Leinsdorf had come to the Met as an assistant conductor, but assistant conductors were basically accompanists for rehearsals, coaches for the singers, and they cued in backstage choruses or on-stage orchestras, such as the band on stage in "Don Giovanni." He was, however, the most talented on the staff, and it did not take him long to be recognized as such.

In the season of 1938-39 when Bodanzky was rehearsing "Die Meistersinger," he did not feel strong enough to do the first act and he invited (although Bodanzky did not invite — he ordered) Leinsdorf to conduct it. Leinsdorf read through the score like a veteran.

He conducted the overture, but then, as he got along during the first act, which is seventy or eighty minutes long, he came to one small passage that was in 6/8 time and the orchestra just seemed to fall apart. He could not conduct so we could follow him. It was the only time I recall that Maestro Leinsdorf faltered.

Bodanzky came down to the edge of the pit and showed him how to handle this very tricky spot.

In those days the operas flew by. We played an opera one week and it went on the shelf. Then if it was an unpopular opera you did not get to play it for weeks at a time. I did not know the scores too well then and we were rehearsing "Die Walkure." The opening is a furious storm scene. The sound is enormous, shattering, and for a number of pages the music reflects this.

Leinsdorf's first rehearsal was on the roof stage of the Met. He was a man of medium height, rather long arms, at least it seemed so to me, and wore a white turtle-neck woolen sweater. There were no nylon sweaters in those days, and when he began to conduct — he had the energy of five people. He did not stop for a second, and all of a sudden as he conducted he shouted notes mostly at the brass and woodwinds. "B flat, F natural, G, A sharp."

Later he stopped and said, "Gentlemen. These notes were incorrectly played." They had escaped the notice of other conductors, but he found corrections to make in the parts that had been incorrectly copied from the score. Maestro Bodanzky, who could not resist glancing at the score to verify, came up to the podium to check. It was comparable to a great athlete setting a new record. Leinsdorf's turtle-neck sweater was drenched by this time.

We were amazed at his knowledge, and he won the orchestra's respect immediately. Leinsdorf had studied the score, and knew it thoroughly. He conducted it with a vicious authority and energy, and the men were astonished. This also inspired us to sit on the edge of our chairs and give the best we could because we knew we were not dealing with a man who was going to pacify us and say, "Okay, gentlemen, on to the next number."

Word spread rapidly about this gifted young conductor who arrived just as Bodanzky was retiring because of illness. Fortunately, Leinsdorf was a quick study who was able to handle the German repertoire extremely well. This included all the Wagner operas we were performing that season: the four Ring cycle operas, for example, along with "Meistersinger," "Lohengrin," "Tannhauser," "Parsifal," "Flying Dutchman," and the three Richard Strauss operas — "Der Rosenkavalier," "Electra" and "Salome." It seems he was willing to undertake this tremendous challenge and did so with success, although that success was the result of his sparing no one and driving the musicians and singers constantly.

No doubt many resented his fastidious and compulsive approach. Many feared him because he never hesitated to criticize or correct any member of the orchestra. But he was getting wonderful results. It was an era in opera that would catapult Leinsdorf to the heights as one of the world's leading conductors.

Leinsdorf left the Met to enter the United States Army in World War II. His next position was as conductor of the Cleveland Symphony. By now he was recognized throughout the world as a fine conductor and guest-conducted many major symphonies. He became conductor of the Rochester Philharmonic Orchestra — a fine symphony orchestra but not one of the nation's major ones. It had a small budget and not enough money to engage players and soloists to play the kind of compositions Leinsdorf wished to present.

He came back to the Metropolitan Opera when Mitropoulos became ill. Mitropoulos was scheduled to record Verdi's "Macbeth" with Maria Callas, but because of contractual difficulties with her, Bing brought in Leonie Rysanek, who had already made a triumphant debut in San Francisco.

She recorded the opera with Leinsdorf as conductor. He was back on the Met roster, taking over a great deal of repertoire that Mitropoulos was scheduled to handle. In addition, Leinsdorf was assigned certain operas agreeable to him and to management — operas he had never conducted before at the Met, such as "Carmen" and "Madame Butterfly."

He remained some four years. I do not think he was very happy to continue beyond that. Leinsdorf was looking for another position. Stiedry was still at the Met and Leinsdorf knew he was a much better conductor than Stiedry. And as do most conductors, he wanted a symphony orchestra position, preferably with one of the Big Five.

His chance came when Charles Munch was about to retire from the Boston Symphony. Leinsdorf was engaged to replace him. When he left Boston after seven or eight years, he guest-conducted all over the world. He came back yet again to the Met in the early 80's to conduct a new "Ring" cycle. This was now the time when James Levine was in full control of artistic matters and virtually everything else. The management would not meet Leinsdorf's requests for more rehearsal time, and I do not think the competition with Levine pleased him either. He has not returned since.

Leinsdorf was a quick study and because of his vast knowledge we never thought of him as being a young conductor. We respected him as a mature conductor, because of the way he held the orchestra together and also because he knew what he wanted and was able to get it from us.

I became friendly with Erich socially because we were both young and unattached, as was a young German friend of his in the orchestra, Werner Lywen, and our first violist, John DiJanni. Erich had more time than we did as he did not have as many performances during the week, so he pursued his other interests, one of which was women.

He was a very attractive young man — he had hair in those days — and was an up and coming conductor. The young singers and ballet dancers all had an eye for him. I remember one soprano, an understudy for starring roles, who would have given her all to have some attention from Erich. She became very frustrated about her career at the Met, for she was still an understudy after six or seven years, and so she left to head the Singing Department of the Toronto Conservatory.

Once, about 1940, we were in Boston on tour, Erich had a brief but intense relationship with one of the ballerinas. Apparently, it did not last long, but she was not ready when he wanted to end it. We were presenting "Carmen," and in the middle of the first act when the mezzo was singing the famous "Habanera" we saw a shoe thrown from the stage. It was aimed at Leinsdorf, and we all ducked, including Leinsdorf, and it sailed out into the audience where a listener took it home as a souvenir. It was like catching a foul ball at Yankee Stadium. But this was no accident. It was aimed by the spurned dancer directly at Erich. She had a good shot at him because of the shallow pit and was so enraged at him that she threw it hoping to eliminate him and her competition at the same time.

As Leinsdorf's ability and popularity with the public and his importance to the Metropolitan Opera grew, the politics of the organization began to surface. Singers took sides. Melchior and Flagstad and a few others felt this was the time to press for their own favorite conductor.

Melchior, in particular, leaned towards Fritz Reiner, who at that time was the conductor of the Pittsburgh Symphony Orchestra. He persuaded Flagstad to side with him. Together, they insisted that the Met engage Reiner. As time passed the issue became very important to them, and they announced via the press that unless the management engaged Reiner, Melchior and Flagstad would not sing that evening at the performance of "Gotterdammerung."

The New York Times carried the announcement on its front page. The newspapers were filled with all kinds of commentary pro and con about this battle. Many people who were not even interested became aware of the so-called feud.

However, Melchior and Flagstad did come to the Met to sing; it's just that no-one knew whether they would finish the opera. Leinsdorf was conducting, and after the first act, there was mild applause for Melchior and thunderous applause for Leinsdorf as he left the pit. To Melchior's astonishment, at his second bow the applause turned to booing. This was instigated by the orchestra, and I am afraid I had a hand in this. I signaled the oboist to let out a raspberry sound by pitching his instrument reed a certain way, which he did, and it rang out through the house, and the orchestra members stamped their feet and booed.

It caught on and a large part of the audience joined us. As a result, the stampede lasted almost as long as the second act, which was an hour long, and extended our salary into overtime.

We were all selfish. Melchior wanted his own man, which would have relegated Leinsdorf to second place, and Erich was not happy about slowing the rapid rise in his career. The orchestra was very prejudiced; we wanted Reiner kept out of the organization. We felt Leinsdorf was the lesser of two evils. Reiner's reputation was that of a tyrant, his disposition, his mannerisms — the orchestra wanted no part of him.

Our demonstration resulted in a quick conference backstage between Melchior and his advisors and David Sarnoff, at that time President of the Board of the Met. They realized that more harm than good would be done by trying to achieve their personal goals, so before the second act began, a strange group came in front of the curtain: Erich Leinsdorf in tails, a man

BEHIND THE GOLD CURTAIN 25

about five feet nine or ten inches, David Sarnoff, a little taller, dressed in tuxedo, and Lauritz Melchior, this giant of a man, in full costume as Siegfried, leopard skin and all. Sarnoff stood between them clasping their hands. He made a speech telling the audience that the stories in the press were exaggerated, and the disagreement was not temperament but tempi. All was well, and they shook hands to prove it.

This pushed Leinsdorf's career forward, and Melchior maintained his importance to the organization, for he had no competition anyway. Leinsdorf became the leading conductor in charge of the German repertoire.

Reiner did come to the Met eventually in the early 1950's, so our campaign worked for more than ten years.

Orchestra Life

The principal singers, both male and female, and conductors had no relationship with the musicians in the orchestra. They were very aloof and played the prima-donna roles to the hilt. There was none of the camaraderie that exists among colleagues today.

However, you could always find someone among the foreign musicians who was friendly with some of the artists. If it was an Italian member of the orchestra, he knew some of the singers from Italy and would exchange news from home, often about relatives from one side of the Aegean or Adriatic. I had no such connections, and except for some of the younger conductors such as Erich Leinsdorf, who was unmarried at the time (as two or three of the musicians were also), we did not socialize very much.

My only concern was the music and the opera. The older members who already knew the repertoire were relaxed, but when the rehearsal was over, I left to go home to practice. If I stayed in the city between rehearsals and performances, I found a corner some place to practice. That was my daily routine.

In the spring of 1938, we had a so-called Spring Season. It was experimental, to see if the public would support a longer season. There were four weeks of opera, from the popular repertoire and occasionally — a premiere. One of these was an opera by Walter Damrosch called "A Man Without A Country." I had played under Damrosch in 1929 as a student delegate to an All-City High School Orchestra in Atlantic City. He was the most prominent conductor in America at that time, and it was a great honor to have been chosen. Damrosch did a great deal to promote classical music in this country via a series of very popular radio broadcasts.

As he was the first famous conductor I had performed with I was very enthusiastic about working with him again now that I was a professional.

Unfortunately, his opera lacked the greatness of a Beethoven or Mozart opera and did not survive its debut season. By now, I had worked with great conductors such as Artur Bodanzky, Fausto Cleva, Sir Thomas Beecham and others, and as time passed I realized that some of the stories I had heard about Damrosch since I had played with him in 1929 were sadly true. The other musicians said, for example, that he conducted superficially. He had a reasonably good baton, they said, but he did not know the music very well, and all nuance was lost. There was a song about him from the last movement of the Fourth Symphony of Tchaikowsky. The rhythm of the phrase was dadadadada-dada-da-da. The musicians sang "Everybody knows it but Damrosch." However, no conductor knows all of the repertoire, and Damrosch earned his reputation fairly. He did more to promote opera, especially German opera, in this country than anyone and made a great contribution to the musical life here. He enjoyed the esteem of the public until his death.

Though ill-fated, Damrosch's opera did serve to introduce a few new young singers. One of them was Helen Traubel. She had long flowing hair, was well built, and very attractive. She became the star of the show. I lost track of her for about five years, until she came back to the Met to replace Kirsten Flagstad, who had to return to Norway during the war. Traubel became a mainstay of the Wagnerian repertoire.

As I began to feel more sure of myself and the opera began to take shape in my mind, I came to appreciate what opera was all about. I enjoyed the singing and started to recognize one voice from another. It became a game and aroused my curiosity to see if I had guessed the name of the performer correctly. I would stand up in the pit during pauses in my music to see who was singing. I had to learn the difference between a mezzo-soprano and a soprano, a basso and a bass-baritone, as I had no experience with singing previously.

I also came to know the different categories of singers, such as stars, prima-donnas, and comprimarios (who do all the small solo roles that supplement the acting, i.e. the maid, the nurse, the guard, the jailer). These are very important to the operas, and the comprimario must know many, many roles in many operas. Most of them were young American singers who came to the opera house directly from the conservatories. They were paid very little, but there was no other place to train in America.

If they were not at the Met they would have had to go to Europe to study, and it was complicated then. There was the expense, where to go, with whom to study, lack of management and so forth. They were delighted to be engaged by the Met for the prestige and the training opportunities. Some of the many singers from that time are Maxine Stillman, who often sang as many as six times a week, and Lucille Browning.

Three new violists — Frank Clawson, Henry Aaron and Paul Bennett — had come into the viola section by this time. They were all Americans, and we soon became good friends. I became especially close to Frank Clawson, who sat with me through many performances. There were a few new members in the cello section, too. Ralph Oxman, a fine cellist, replaced an 80-year-old who had long been due for retirement. There were some new bass players. One was Sam Goldman, a graduate of Juilliard who suddenly and mysteriously resigned. We found out later he went to California because he could not handle the stress of the job.

There were other changes, primarily American performers replacing retirees who were mostly European. It was the beginning of the war and times were difficult. Unless they had to, most people did not resign. You played a job until you could no longer play or you were released.

The Juilliard School was closely associated with the Met in those days and gave the opera a great deal of money. Whenever there was an opening, the school sent its people over. However, there was not any wholesale clean-up until 1936-1937; the management had discussed it with the conducting staff, who decided to re-audition all the string players.

That was just before I came in, so I did not know the politics of the organization. I understand the orchestra tried to get support from Local 802 to avoid this, but it lost the case, and everybody in the string sections had to audition.

One or two members refused: they were not re-engaged. I recall one man in particular was a very fine violinist. A man of principle, he would not audition. He suffered as a result. Others were re-admitted.

After all, a man who had been in the orchestra thirty or forty years — especially in an opera orchestra with its brutal schedule and highly specialized repertoire, was not always able to keep up the pace. It was not like being a young soloist straight out of the Juilliard. An audition was nerve-wracking, so I can safely say that many of them must have suffered terribly. And it was probably Artur Bodanzky's idea. He had the greatest influence.

Up to thirty percent of the orchestra had been replaced in 1936, so the pace was much slower. Three violas were added. One who had left was my friend, David Dawson. He had a reputation as a soloist and played with the small symphony orchestras on Long Island and other places.

Dawson was a big gangling guy from West Virginia, near Wheeling, and was considered one of the most talented violists in New York City. Very conscientious, very serious, he practiced every minute. Towards the end of the season he was engaged as a soloist somewhere in Freeport, Long Island. I was still playing with the string quartet and the three other members of the quartet were playing this job in Freeport. I could not play that performance as I had a matinee that day, so when the performance was over, Dawson came to me and asked what his colleagues thought of his performance.

They had already told me what they thought, but I was not about to tell him. Well, he hounded me until I finally gave in. They said, basically, that he was a fine player, but that he sounded very tired and made errors in intonation, and had memory slips. He took their criticism very seriously and made up his mind to leave the Met as soon as he could. The schedule was just too demanding and he wanted to pursue a solo career and knew he could not do this with the twenty-four hour commitment needed at the Met. When Mitropoulos went to Minneapolis as conductor, he went with him as First Violist.

The tour that year was three weeks long. The tours began to increase in length and this was our opportunity to become acquainted with the rest of the company, the dancers, chorus, solo singers, etc. There were few rehearsals, and long hours on the trains. Also, I was much more comfortable. I was getting to learn more and more of the operation of the opera. I wanted to know what made the opera "tick." Why was it so popular, and why was the public so enamored of the stars, why did people prefer some performances to others?

The trips bi-weekly to Philadelphia and Baltimore, and the long tours to Texas and California gave me the opportunity to sort out the various members of the company. The democratic spirit came to the fore, and I began to discover who people were and what their duties were at the opera. I found that many of them had the same problems I had in the beginning. They were not able to figure out who was who and what was what. All were concerned with their own problems — to learn the job and produce well. Everyone was under pressure.

The tours offered the opportunity to meet singers and all kinds of workers, such as wig-makers, make-up people, costumers, stage-hands, in addition to the orchestra members.

In those days we traveled in Pullman cars. Everyone had either an upper or lower berth, and there was no place to meet except in dining cars. There were no parlor cars. Usually the scenario was as follows: about one hundred members of the company waiting for breakfast, lunch, or dinner, lined up through the cars. We stood in the aisles next to the people who stayed put because they were smart enough to have brought their own food. They were not at all concerned about the dining-car seating.

We younger men never thought of such a practical solution. We awoke about eight, stood in the hot aisles to get into the hot dining-car. There was no air-conditioning, just fans, and they usually broke down somewhere along the line. We got the second-rate trains for these tours; the good ones went on regular passenger runs.

The cooling system was the best there was at the time. Huge blocks of ice were in compartments under the cars, fans blew over the ice into vents to cool the cars. We stopped often for the train personnel to inspect these compartments, to drain them, to see if there was ice left and to check if the fans worked, as they often did not.

When my turn came after an hour and a half wait, it was my good fortune to be seated at a table with Edward Johnson, the General Manager of the company, another member of the orchestra and the great Ezio Pinza. We sat facing one another and the conversation began haltingly. I thought of these people as gods and I was very shy. Johnson was very personable and democratic. He spoke to everyone on an equal basis and wanted to know everyone's thoughts about the opera and other matters. He always acted with everyone's interests at heart. The morning's conversation led to a series of story-telling and jokes, and though I was still in awe of him, I saw that Ezio Pinza was human, like me. He was considerably taller than I. He was also exceptionally handsome, and more relaxed. He was one of the greatest stars in a period of legendary opera stars, the most important basso in the Italian as well as the French repertoire. He always played the sinister villain in the Verdi operas, the patient kindly father in "Louise" of G. Charpentier, the vengeful lover in "Manon" and Mephisto in "Faust."

His English was awful! What I could understand was broken, bent, and battered. He really assaulted the language with his strong accent, though he had been in the United States for perhaps nine seasons; it's just that with his hectic schedule he had no time to study English formally. He was able to make himself understood with yes, no, and body English. And he certainly had learned to count, as he was the best paid star in the company.

At last it was my turn to tell a story, and I did not know what kind of story to tell because I did not feel at ease. I did not think I could tell him an off-color story, but I did anyway. I thought of a puzzle that was shown to me years before by my friend Morton Gould. It was a visual joke and I wrote it on a napkin because I could not find a piece of paper. (The table linen was so beautiful in those days on the Pullman trains, it was like writing on parchment.) It looked like hieroglyphics, constructed on numbers inverted. If you turned it upside down it became quite legible and spelled out an off-color story. Edward Johnson read it first and howled with laughter; Pinza, naturally, wanted to see it too, and he too collapsed with laughter. He became my instant friend and asked me to make a few copies. There I was, eating my breakfast, drinking my coffee, and making copies of this silly joke on beautiful damask linen napkins. From that time on, Pinza and I were friends.

Singers

Ezio Pinza was an extraordinary personality. He was one of the most natural actors on the opera stage, and he was a great basso. He was not concerned with the problems most singers have — voice production, memorization of words and music. His concern was his ability to create the character he played.

That was very unusual at the time, as most singers more or less gestured, stood and sang. The stars created their own movements and staging. They had to follow a certain pattern since they had to be in the right spot on the stage if they were singing a duet or serenading the chorus or a group of comprimarios. But when Pinza sang a duet or a solo to a woman, his lovemaking projected to every woman in the audience.

In Mozart's opera "Don Giovanni," he played the title role to the hilt. He would make love to Zerlina or Donna Anna, and his acting was so intense he would not face the audience. There were various reasons for this, especially if it was a scene where he had to pour out his love from the heart. If there was not too much movement in the scene, he would hold the hand of the soprano, gently massage her fingers, grab the other arm to circumvent resistance, placing it behind her, and often under her skirt. He often wandered about the stage, and in full view of the audience his hands wandered, too, often under a layer or two of costume.

He had no compunction about it, as the soprano, mezzo-soprano, the soloists and also female chorus members were prisoners. They could not very well protest while they were singing. Often husbands or boyfriends were sitting in the audience, and the protests came after the performance. The orchestra could see this, but the public could not, they thought it was just great acting.

Elizabeth Rethberg was brought to this country in the late 20's. We later heard that Pinza and Rethberg had quite a romance going. Rethberg was not married (I do not think she had ever been married at that point). She was deeply in love with Pinza, but Pinza was still married to an Italian woman he had left in Italy.

Rethberg was brought to the Met primarily to sing Mozart, but her repertoire was so extensive, she sang the Wagner roles with Flagstad, and also the Italian dramatic repertoire. The first time I heard her, she sang Desdemona in "Othello" and the title role in "Aida." I wondered if there was anything she could not perform. As a young member of the company I was amazed that she sang half the repertoire we were presenting at the time — the season of 1937-38.

As to her acting, I am not qualified to judge since in those early days I was too busy watching my music to observe her. I venture to say it was mediocre, as she was a rather large woman, rotund, yet with a beautiful face. She always had a warm smile, a charming personality, and a dignified manner. Pinza and Rethberg gave joint recitals, and traveled together all over the United States. The affair, which was common knowledge, lasted until the 1940's. She retired from the Met, and sang only solo recitals and with symphony orchestras.

Lauritz Melchior was known as our most important helden-tenor. He had a big voice that carried over the orchestra, a large range, and incredible endurance. He sang all the important Wagner roles. It did not take me long to realize he was not only a fine singer, but a man made of steel. He sang an average of four performances a week — everything in the Wagner repertoire, Lohengrin, Tannhauser, Siegfried in the "Ring."

Most of the foreign singers were friendly, especially Melchior. He was nice to everyone, from the porters and ushers to the maestros. He knew some of the older members of the orchestra on a first-name basis, but as a young man I was always afraid to approach the stars. All I could do was applaud, just as the public did.

My first encounter with Melchior was on a trip to Philadelphia. We went there every other week by train, about a two-hour run. Melchior was an avid bridge player as was his wife, and she usually traveled with him. She was petite and he always called her "Shatzie." They were looking for a pair of bridge players on this trip, and delegated Artur Bodanzky — our most important conductor — to commandeer two orchestra members. He came through the cars of the orchestra looking for two bridge players, stopping short at my compartment.

I was chatting with our solo trumpet player, Isadore Blank; Bodanzky knew him well. He knew all the brass players by name, but he did not know me at the time. This was really the first time I had spoken to Bodanzky personally. He asked if I could come to Melchior's compartment along with Blank to play bridge. Blank volunteered immediately, and tried to persuade me to join him. You did not say no to Bodanzky, so while I protested that I did not play very well, I was pushed into going with them. I was so nervous, I had the shakes as though I were playing a big solo. We marched through two cars, sat down, were introduced to Mr. and Mrs. Melchior and we played bridge. I do not recall the score, but I am sure I was the worst player of the group. However, we kept the game going and I suppose as with most card players, the less proficient I was, the more proficient Melchior appeared, and he enjoyed it because he won every round. When we arrived in Philadelphia, we disembarked, and Izzy Blank and I went to dinner.

The performance that night was either "Siegfried" or "Gotterdammerung," and Melchior sang the role of Siegfried. It was held at the Philadelphia Academy of Music. Acoustically it was a wonderful hall, but poorly equipped for opera or ballet. The stage was inadequate and the pit was worse. We had to squeeze in and dodge the bows and trombone slides of the other players.

Melchior was over six feet tall, a giant of a man. In this particular role, he wore a leopard skin draped over him like a toga, and with his long legs, hairy and skinny, and his long arms sticking out too, he looked like Tarzan of the jungle. He also wore a wig, and carried a sword and a club.

After the first act, he came rushing down under the stage, through the corridor where they stored the scenery. There were fifty or sixty orchestra members lounging around there between the acts, and when they saw Melchior heading for the pit in full costume and make-up they followed him. They had never seen a singer do this.

He asked one of the men he knew, "Can you tell me vere is dat tall, dark musician. I must see him immediately!" He spoke English quite well with a heavy Danish accent, with a little British mixed in, but he was easy to understand. Finally, he spotted me talking with a group of men and approached.

Everybody turned in his direction to see what it was he wanted. They thought he was coming down to beat somebody up. He looked ferocious in that leopard skin and make-up, and he did not approach me very gently either. Rather, he came at me as though he were going to attack. However, he simply pointed at me and said, "You! Vould you please come to our compartment after the opera, and ve vill continue our game. Ve had a vonderful time, and tell your colleague Mr. Blank to come vid you."

Gladys Swarthout was a mezzo-soprano who was strikingly attractive. She sang roles like "Carmen" and Delilah in "Samson and Delilah," and was well-known to the American public because of her radio broadcasts.

Her early training was probably in musical comedy, and she knew one thing — how to upstage everyone. She had a walk that we called "swivel-hips" and used it to advantage. The stage directors in those days were as well-versed as they are today, but they did not have the authority that stage directors exercise in today's productions. The stars were free spirits, and were permitted to do the role any way they wished.

There was a famous Polish tenor then, Jan Kiepura, who was as adept as Swarthout at upstaging other performers. When she sang "Carmen" to his "Don José" they would start somewhere in the back of the stage and inevitably wind up at the footlights regardless of the action. They were severely criticized for this behavior as performances were supposed to be group performances, not individual acts with back-up. Still, it continued. I heard that in a performance of "Carmen" in Pittsburgh he kicked her in the shins, causing her to fall down and break her leg. That was the last time they sang together. They were mortal enemies from that time on.

Kirsten Flagstad was the greatest Wagnerian soprano of that time or since; certainly the greatest Isolde in "Tristan and Isolde." She had an angelic face, but was a very heavy-set woman. Her cheeks were always creased in a smile. She was built the way we were led to believe a Wagnerian heroine was built — straight up and down, no waist, just bulk.

But looks or size did not mean much then; it was a question of whether or not a singer could survive the performance of these difficult and long operas. Flagstad had tremendous stamina. She sang as many as four times a week like Melchior, and the sound was always beautiful. The more the conductor asked for a crescendo or fortissimo, the more her voice soared above the orchestra and filled the auditorium. As I sat in the pit that voice became more familiar than anyone else's. I recognized it instantly.

Later I began to glance at the stage to watch her more closely. She would stand in one spot, especially as Isolde, and just pour out that magnificent sound. It was unforgettable.

The only personal contact I had with her was the time I walked with her from Penn Station in Philadelphia to the Academy of Music. It was a winter day, with slush on the ground. No limousine for Flagstad; she walked, with her accompanist Edwin McArthur, and another singer. We walked four abreast making small talk. Again, I found the goddess was human, very friendly and unassuming.

A year or two later on the occasion of her twenty-fifth anniversary as a singer at the Met, she endeared herself to the company even more. Not every star was always gracious and not every star recognized their colleagues the way Flagstad did. A party was held in the Sherry Lounge at the Old Met for the company, given after one of her performances. The food, the hors d'oeuvres and champagne flowed like Niagara Falls. This was my first experience with this kind of service. I sat at a table with some of my colleagues and two waiters were assigned to each table, one to bring food, and the other to watch the champagne glasses empty and to replenish them promptly. The champagne was Mumm's, the best, and I had four or five glasses — another new experience. I thought champagne was carbonated grape juice, and I soon felt the effects. I forgot where I was sitting and whose party it was. I did know I had an hour and a half trip to get home to Long Island.

I still do not know how I got there. But I did, and I still do not know how I managed to get up to go to rehearsal the next morning. It took me five days to get rid of the hang-over. I learned in one painful lesson, however, that four or five glasses of champagne can do much more damage than four or five scotches.

When Flagstad came back to the United States in the 1955 season after the war, she was no longer the singer we had heard before. Then, too, there were many anti-Nazi demonstrations against her appearances, because her husband was accused of being a Quisling. She sang with us for one or two years. She had come primarily to see her daughter who had married an American and settled somewhere in the midwest.

Lily Pons was a very big star at the Metropolitan in those days. She was a tiny will-of-the-wisp, very dainty, weighing about a hundred pounds. She came from the Paris Opera with no particular reputation, but there was a need for a fine coloratura at the Met, and she became the most popular coloratura we had.

Her repertoire was tremendous — "Lakme," "Rigoletto," "Lucia di Lammermoor," all the coloratura roles. She wanted to sing more dramatic roles such as Violetta in "La Traviata," but management did not permit it. It was the era of Licia Albanese and others who sang that sort of role more effectively.

My contact with Pons was minimal. I made a few recordings with her outside the Met. She had married Andre Kostelanetz, the popular conductor and arranger, and they made many recordings together. They were very successful commercially; we spoke together occasionally during those sessions.

However, there were stories about her frugality — she knew how to squeeze a buck. Once at a rehearsal of one of her operas, I was amazed to see that she walked in wearing a magnificent mink coat, and those were the days when only very wealthy people could afford this. She was late that day and instantly walked on stage, dropping this valuable coat on the dirty stage floor. She began to sing, and slowly peeled off the white gloves she was wearing. There was a hole worn in every finger!

Rise Stevens came to the Metropolitan Opera in the 1937-38 or 1938-39 season. There was a lot of hullabaloo and a very big build-up as she was an American singer, a local girl from Jackson Heights, who had made it big in Europe. She had sung in all the important opera houses before she came to the Met, and had married a Czech she met while singing in Prague.

She was immediately catapulted to stardom here. She did a very sexy "Carmen" and also Delilah in "Samson and Delilah" to an extent unknown in this country. I was beginning to spend more time looking at the stage than looking at my parts of the music as I had memorized most of them by now, and whenever Rise Stevens appeared, my eyes popped. Her costumes were unbelievable! As Delilah she wore a bra and short underwear and diaphanous material. This was an unfamiliar sight at the opera as most of the singers had to cover up to hide the bulges. But Rise Stevens, with her singing, her looks, and her ability as an actress had no such qualms. She sang the role of the Bearer of the Rose in "Rosenkavalier," a "pants" role, and in her white satin pants, white wig and silver braid costume, she looked lovely.

Much later on we became friends. Although Gladys Swarthout and Rise Stevens sang approximately the same repertoire, they were not competitors per se. At that time Stevens sang very often — she was a regular staff artist, while Swarthout was more or less a guest star, as she was making movies and singing on radio.

I was aware now that the activity around me was an important part of the show, and I became very interested in the German wing of the opera. In those early days playing an opera by Wagner was a great challenge for me, and I believed that this was the kind of music that would keep me in shape as an instrumentalist. It was very difficult — although I also acknowledged that it represented some of the greatest music written. I later changed my views on that subject because "La Traviata" or any of the Verdi or Puccini operas are artistically just as great as a Wagner "Tannhauser." The so-called simpler operas that constituted a large part of the Metropolitan Opera repertoire were, in their own way, as great and as important to this art form as any Wagner opera.

However, at that period in my career my main interest was in observing, listening, and playing German opera. I came to know most of the singers casually — some better than others. The ones I knew best were the ones who sang most frequently with the company. At that time, singers sang the same role repeatedly during a season.

A man like Emanuel List, for example, was known as our greatest basso in Wagnerian roles. He sang Hunding and Wotan in "The Ring" and since we also performed Richard Strauss operas often, he sang the role of Baron von Ochs in "Der Rosenkavalier" for almost all the performances. He was a fine singer, and like many of the artists, had been well established as a great performer before he ever reached the Met. But after awhile, he began to fade, and he was replaced by younger singers who knew the same roles.

Freidrich Schorr was another great baritone in German roles. Unfortunately, I did not have the good luck to hear him in his prime during the 1920's, but I heard enough of him as Hans Sachs in "Die Meistersinger" to know that he was a great singer; watching him on the stage, you could see he was entirely at home.

Then we had a great Scandinavian contralto, Karen Branzell. She had been in the company before Flagstad, Thorberg and the rest, and many people thought she was an American.

When she sang a role with the Met, no one ever had to worry about the voice carrying. It rose to the rafters and blew the roof off. Her voice was beautiful, but I recall too the distinctive quality of the sound. It boomed like a cannon.

The Metropolitan Opera House in New York, even the Old Met, is either the first or second largest in the world. I think the Opera Colon in Buenos Aires had a few more seats. Most singers could not fill a house like the Met with normal voice production. The singers who had great success in Europe sang in 1,500 seat auditoriums like the Vienna Opera House or La Scala, while the Met seats 4,000. These singers were very successful on their own territory, but when they came to the Met, their voices had to be forced to fill the auditorium, and this changed the quality of the voice. The critics picked it up, and unfortunately, many careers were ruined in America; these artists had to return to Europe.

A few had the ability to fill the auditorium with sound, and we thought of them as having been born to sing at a house like the Met. Branzell, Flagstad and Melchior were this type of singer. They had enormous voices and, for the Wagner "Ring," that was what was required because the orchestration was twice as heavy as that of the Italian operas.

Kirsten Thorberg was one of the finest artists in the house. She usually sang with Flagstad, the role of Brangaene in "Tristan and Isolde" and whenever she was needed she sang in the Italian operas. She had a great range, and sang many mezzo-soprano roles, too. She performed in many of the early productions of the Gluck operas such as "Orpheus and Eurydice." Thorberg also sang Amneris in "Aida" and other mezzo-soprano roles.

She was a very statuesque woman and when she sang in "Orpheus and Eurydice" dressed in the Greek costume of the period, with a band on her head, and a short skirt, strumming her lyre, she was most imposing. Whenever a singer wore a short skirt, at intermission the conversation by the musicians, mostly men at that time, was how we enjoyed seeing her in the short skirt. After all it was more pleasant to see an attractive singer dressed like that than some of the others who were built like tanks.

Lawrence Tibbett was becoming a legend at the Metropolitan Opera. He was an American singer, and the management team of Johnson and Ziegler was American and they favored American singers. They loved Tibbett because he was the number one box office attraction. Every time he appeared, the Met was sold out. Many new productions were created for him such as "Simon Boccanegra" and "Rigoletto," two of his most famous interpretations.

Tibbett left an important legacy as he was instrumental in the original organization of AGMA — the American Guild of Musical Artists, the union for solo instrumentalists, singers, chorus, and ballet. However, social life was also intriguing to him and I soon realized he drank considerably. There were many occasions when he was not able to sing his best, and it got progressively worse.

Once when we were on tour, he was so drunk that with the assistance of a few of my colleagues, I had to carry him to his hotel to sleep it off. He was replaced that night by an understudy, much to the disappointment of the audience. His bad personal habits definitely shortened his career, as singers must keep in good physical condition, and he did nothing to preserve his voice.

Nino Martini was a handsome tenor who was brought in to sing at the Met primarily because of his popularity on a Sunday radio program he did with Andre Kostelanetz for the Coca-Cola Company. It was not fair to judge anyone's voice operatically via radio, but on radio he impressed me as being a fine artist with a beautiful sound. However, when he sang at the Met, I was very disappointed. He had a very small voice. I could not hear him most of the time. In addition he had great difficulty with intonation. This was the first time I had ever heard a singer with this problem; unfortunately, it was not the last. I presume this was again the result of trying to fill a huge house. He had to force the voice to be heard at all, and this created all sorts of vocal problems. He did not last very long, perhaps two to four seasons. He later invested his money very well in a Catskill mountain lodge and that is where he finished his career — as a country gentleman.

Giovanni Martinelli came to the Met in the twenties when Caruso and Gigli were there. When I came to the opera, he was our most important dramatic tenor in the Italian and French repertoire. His repertoire was vast and he even sang a few German operas. He was Radames in "Aida" and sang the title role in "Othello."

When I met up with him, Martinelli had become an American citizen and was a mainstay at the opera. I later discovered that only tenors who were not afraid of splitting their vocal cords would attempt "Othello." Only a mature artist would sing that role. Martinelli no longer had the beautiful quality he may have had in earlier years. He was a "belter," and his voice had a gruff quality — he bellowed. There were parts of the range in his voice that did not have the resonance one likes to hear in a tenor. His career lasted well into the 40's — an extraordinary length of time for a singer.

More About Conductors

When I joined the opera orchestra in 1936, my career turned in a direction I had not anticipated. I had thought in terms of following a career as a chamber music artist or soloist, or possibly joining the New York Philharmonic as many of my friends and colleagues from the New York Philharmonic Scholarships had done. However, in the 1930's the economic situation was bad, and orchestra musicians were poorly paid. Therefore, when I was offered the Metropolitan Opera position, I was pleased, as it paid much more than any other orchestra position.

Many prominent guest conductors were invited to conduct new productions. We all looked forward to playing with these great men as a new conductor always presented a challenge. At that time, Sir Thomas Beecham, one of the most famous in the world, came to the Metropolitan Opera and stayed from 1939 to 1942.

Beecham was notorious for his acid wit and his sarcastic comments, but he was usually very nice to us. He had a clipped upper-class British accent, and always had something amusing to say about things that had nothing to do with the orchestra. It was usually some withering comment regarding the production.

The repertoire assigned to him was "Carmen" and "Faust" and a few other operas. On one occasion, he criticized the women of the chorus for falling behind in the music, and one of them said, "But Maestro, we cannot move about in these costumes and also see your beat."

It was a new production of "Faust." The costumes had hoop skirts, and both the costumes and choristers were very heavy. The stage director, Desire Defrere, demanded more physical action, and the chorus simply could not oblige: they could not act and watch Beecham, too.

Beecham stopped the rehearsal after hearing the complaint and said,

"Well, get rid of them. Have new ones made. I'll take care of the expense."

And he could. He was one of the heirs to the family fortune amassed from Beecham's Little Liver Pills, one of the most popular patent medicines of the time and his fortune helped his career.

Beecham was a fine symphony conductor, but he was competent, not great, as an opera conductor; he did not have too much experience. He did not know people at the Met by name or who directed what and one day when things were not going well, he yelled, "Who's the bloomin' idjet giving the cues backstage and handling the chorus?"

Out in front of the curtain stepped our chorus master at the time, Fausto Cleva. His English was poor then, but he knew from the tone of the voice that he was being insulted, even more so after his Italian friends explained what Beecham had said. Cleva left shortly after that and went on to become one of the most famous opera conductors in the world.

On one of our monthly visits to Philadelphia, Beecham was scheduled to conduct. This was immediately prior to our entry into World War II and it was customary to play the Star Spangled Banner before each performance. Everyone (including the audience) stood except the cellists, and all joined in the singing. We had rehearsed and played our anthem many times, so we assumed that Beecham knew it. I have not been able to determine to this day if it was deliberate or due to ignorance, but he conducted the anthem at more than twice the speed it was supposed to be, and of course as good orchestra men, we followed him.

When we had finished, the audience was more than half way back in the anthem. They continued to sing to the bitter end, and did not even notice that the orchestra had finished. Beecham stood there looking down at the floor, waiting for the audience to finish. We were all embarrassed, he most of all, but he was not going to admit it so he said, "What's the matter with these bloomin' idjets? Don't they know their own national anthem?"

Before he came to conduct us, we had heard he occasionally would single out one person and correct him with scathing sarcasm. As it turned out, he may have told someone he wanted a passage played in a particular way, but he never humiliated any of us. He was very professional, mature, in his prime as a conductor.

The arrival of Bruno Walter was eagerly awaited by all of us because his reputation preceded him. He was known world-wide as a great interpreter and had just arrived in America. He eventually settled in California but that was later on. Bruno Walter was invited to the Met to conduct Beethoven's "Fidelio" and also some Mozart operas.

At our first rehearsal of "Fidelio" with him, I was a bit bewildered as I could not follow or understand his beat. I discussed this with my colleagues, those who knew the repertoire better than I did, and they explained that since Walter was more a musical interpreter than a technician, you had to know your own part thoroughly. If I watched him closely, I became very confused. You had to know what you were doing and look at him occasionally to find out where the beat was and what the dynamics were. He put his ideas across to the orchestra by doing a considerable amount of talking and the rest he did with the baton.

The first rehearsal we had with him for Mozart, he raised his baton and was about to conduct the down-beat, but then he put up his left hand to the orchestra, and said, "Gentlemen. It's already too loud." We had not played a note! I later discovered this was one of his funny little tricks to impress the musicians that Mozart had to be subdued unless there was a specific indication for loud playing.

The "Fidelio" was a triumph. The cast was superb, the best that could possibly be assembled — Kirsten Flagstad, Rene Maison, Julius Heuhn, Alexander Kipnis. When we played the first introductory "Fidelio" overture and the one in the second act — the "Leonore" — during the scenery change, the applause for the Maestro was thunderous. We could not continue with the opera for at least fifteen or twenty minutes. The audience was hungry for someone of Walter's calibre, and he had a tremendous following. This performance was one of the great moments in Metropolitan Opera history.

Once when he conducted "Don Giovanni," Ezio Pinza was in the cast. It was rumored that Pinza had had an affair with Bruno Walter's daughter, and Pinza left her flat. We had all heard this sad story and I thought he would be very angry at Pinza and hardly cooperate with him at the opera. I was gravely mistaken. Bruno Walter was very professional and he knew Pinza's ability. He treated him with great courtesy and respect.

The management later asked Walter to conduct "Un Ballo en Maschera" by Verdi. This was the first time since I had been at the Met that I had played the opera. In those days four or five years could pass before we played some of the Verdi operas. I thought these operas just were not very popular. I was wrong. Of course, that was my ignorance. I had been at the opera about fifteen years before I had an opportunity to play Verdi's "La Forza del Destino." Today, because of the length of the season, you can hear one opera twenty times in one year.

Some conductors were specific about what they wanted. They did it with the stick, or told us precisely what they wanted, and at what point in the score. Bruno Walter had his own peculiar mannerisms. He had a way of putting his hand to his heart and seeming to be on the verge of tears as though he were deeply offended at the way we were performing a particular passage. I gather he did this most of his life instead of scolding.

In an important soprano aria in "Un Ballo en Maschera" — the soprano was Zinka Milanov — she was singing way up in her range, and was accompanied by oboe and English horn solos. Walter stopped them two or three times as the intonation between the two instruments was not very good. He put his hand to his heart as though to say "You are making my heart bleed! It should not be this way." The orchestra responded very well to that technique as its members worked harder to please him.

Not every performer pleased every conductor and, as happens in many orchestras, some players are past their prime and do not perform the way they did some years before. This is particularly true of woodwinds. I remember one incident in particular. Walter suggested that the first oboist take over and play the English horn part to end the aria. The English hornist, Josef Marx, was a very fine musician but not a great performer; he could not hit the high note with the appropriate sound.

I was shocked. I did not know if the Union would permit this.

The only time I remember that Bruno Walter offended anyone personally was this incident. However, the impression I got was that Bruno Walter got his way one way or another, or he would go behind your back to management. I may be entirely wrong, but that is the feeling I had about him — that he was not to be trusted entirely.

Some conductors dealt with a problem directly and immediately, whether it was embarrassing to the player or not. Artur Bodanzky was like that. He took it out on you on the spot; at the end of the season he took it out on you permanently. You lost your job.

Other conductors were very happy to be engaged by the Metropolitan Opera, and they were nicer to us than they were to their own orchestras where they were very autocratic. No conductor could get away with this behavior today; the musicians would not tolerate it and the Union would not permit it.

When these guest conductors came to the Met they behaved like human beings, though at home they were absolute dictators. We particularly enjoyed having them as we had one or two of our own who thought we belonged to them and treated us that way. We were always in fear that this could be our last season, and as I mentioned earlier there were no jobs to be had.

Rehearsals & Orchestra Procedure

Unlike the symphony orchestra, musicians of the opera orchestra work under six or seven conductors in a week. Generally, rehearsals — four per week — are for the preparation of operas two weeks in advance of scheduled performances and are conducted by the maestros designated for those operas. Occasionally, another rehearsal would be interspersed for another part of the repertoire.

When I started at the Met, we had eight performances each week, seven nights and a Saturday matinee. In one week you could have two German operas, a French opera or two, and three or four Italian operas. Each one had a different conductor, and each conductor had a different style, different schooling, different abilities.

In addition, there were frequent cast changes because the singers carried a heavy load. Occasionally, the original conductor was called in for a quick run-through for the benefit of the newly assigned singers. This did not happen too often in the early years; because of so many operas in the repertoire and a short season, the time was very limited for rehearsal. In my last twenty years with the Met, however, it was a fairly frequent occurrence, especially in preparation for tours with completely new casts. Obviously, special rehearsals were necessary.

The entire orchestra had to develop a certain flexibility and the Met orchestra was uncanny in this respect. Someone referred to us as an "orchestral rubber band." There were many instances in the early years when we were very tired because of the long and difficult schedule. We were exhausted by the time of the evening performance, and barely glanced at the conductor. Our eyes were only on our parts.

Except me. My mind wandered as I knew most of the repertoire by ear; I simply listened to the singers. I could almost tell, as could many of my colleagues, whether the singer had a good night or a good day or what he or she had eaten. I could tell easily whether a singer was in good voice or not. Generally, this was manifested by idiosyncrasies, such as not being able to hold tempi. If they wanted to get through in a hurry, they sang faster. If the voice was in great shape they held on to a note endlessly. A few of the great stars, who did not care who was conducting, held on to a good high note forever and we went along. If the singer could not hold onto the note for its proper length, generally he or she would just stop singing, and if the conductor was alert enough he would cut us off immediately.

To illustrate the various problems the orchestra had to face with conductors, I can tell you about a Czech conductor brought to the Met on the recommendation of Bruno Walter. His name was Paul Breisach. He had a fine reputation in Europe and was considered a very capable conductor. I knew very little about his personal life, but our rehearsals with him were very well conducted. His repertoire was primarily Czech operas, Smetana's "Bartered Bride," Janacek operas, and also some Mozart. He was a fine musician and everything went well.

We did not know that he imbibed a bit. Actually he imbibed a great deal, and when he came to the evening performance he had to be pointed to the orchestra pit, and helped onto the podium. We did not know what to watch, his baton or his body, because he swayed back and forth. He never knew the difference between the upbeat and the downbeat and the miracle was that we finished the performance in pretty good shape in spite of the conductor. We knew what we were doing, but he was certainly no help to us. The music may have been going through his head, but he had no way of executing the proper movement of his hands to convey his wishes to us. He did not remedy his weakness and did not last long at the Met.

Fritz Reiner was engaged by the Metropolitan Opera about 1948 and stayed with us for about ten years off and on. His reputation was well-established as the conductor of the Pittsburgh Symphony by then and we knew he was very talented and capable. A number of our orchestra members had worked with him in Pittsburgh prior to their Metropolitan Opera engagement: Oscar Voget, violin; Leonard Grossman, viola; Richard Nass, oboe; Jacques Rubenstein, violin; to name a few. When we heard of Reiner's impending arrival at the Met, many musicians were disturbed — especially the older ones. Reiner's "shtick" was to ask individual members of the string sections to stand up and play a passage solo. Some of the older orchestra musicians, though very capable, had not played solo for thirty or forty years. I recall that my partner at the time, who had been in the orchestra for forty or forty-five years, was terrified at the very thought of having to play individually.

In Pittsburgh where he was an absolute ruler he could get away with this behavior, but we were determined to prevent it at the Met. I must explain too that Reiner often used a very short baton and if you sat at the rear of the orchestra, it looked like a toothpick, especially to the bass players who were strung out at the rear of the orchestra pit.

Reiner's technique was precise, using the absolute minimal amount of movement. He sometimes just bent the joints of his fingers with the baton instead of waving it. All you saw was a slight movement, if you were able to see it at all. To cue in the brass he would puff his cheeks in and out to indicate blowing.

There is a famous story about a bass player in the Pittsburgh Symphony who came in to rehearsal with a telescope on a stand which he focused on Reiner's baton. Reiner stopped the rehearsal and said, "Young man, what are you doing?" The bassist answered, "Maestro, I brought the telescope to see your beat better." Reiner was furious and dismissed him on the spot.

When his arrival at the Met was imminent, we had meetings of the orchestra committees to promulgate a course of action for dealing with the Maestro. The woodwinds met separately, and the strings met separately. I was on the committee for the string section. John DiJanni, our first violist, was chairman. We discussed a number of plans and finally decided that should he point out one man of a section to play a passage, we en-masse and without comment, would stand up together and play the passage as one man. If his behavior was tyrannical and ill-tempered, we planned to call on our friend and ally, Al Manuti, the president of Local 802.

One violinist in the orchestra, Daniel Falk, had played with Reiner in Pittsburgh. It is said that Falk warned Reiner of our meetings and plans. On Reiner's arrival to conduct his debut opera with us, "Salome" by Richard Strauss, he came to the first rehearsal, was introduced to us, and though many were very nervous about his stay with us, he greeted us very properly.

Reiner was a man of slow, deliberate speech and had a slight accent. He had already been in the United States for at least twenty-five years. His career had started here at the Curtis Institute in Philadelphia and he went on to the Pittsburgh Symphony. We were surprised to find him quite human. He said, "Good morning, gentlemen," and started the rehearsal.

We could see immediately that the stories we had heard about his baton technique were absolutely true. There was a minimal amount of movement. He had his glasses lowered to the tip of his nose — he obviously did not believe in bifocals — and would look up occasionally from the score.

We discovered he was very well acquainted with the score, which was very difficult. He also proceeded to inform us, as many conductors had done in the past and others would do in the future, that he was a close personal friend of the composer, Richard Strauss. Perhaps as an explanation for his method of conducting he said that Strauss told him that "the goal of every conductor who conducts my scores should be to learn the score so thoroughly that when he conducted the performance his collar should not be wilted." Reiner said, "This, gentlemen, is the case with me. You won't find me in a sweat. I won't get excited. Our purpose is to go through the score as best we can."

In the years he conducted us, I do not recall him ever blowing up at anybody. He never asked any of us to play solo except for the woodwinds, and that is customary. But there was one incident. We had performed Wagner's "The Flying Dutchman" in Philadelphia the previous evening and came home very late. The next morning it was rehearsal as usual. We had not been up to par the evening before, at least in Maestro Reiner's opinion. He insulted the orchestra by calling us "a very bad orchestra." He criticized our playing saying that we played out of tune, we did not follow his beat and so on. We were beginning to know our strength as a unit in those days, so the orchestra committee held a meeting and we insisted he apologize. He did it by repeating the same phrase, and said, "We were not a bad orchestra, we had played like one." Actually, of course, he never apologized, and we did not get the satisfaction we were looking for — nor did he.

Generally, however, Reiner was very nice to the orchestra and when he left us on his appointment as conductor of the Chicago Symphony in the early 50's, he gave a beautiful party for us during our tour when we were in Toronto. It was a mid-afternoon buffet with lots of champagne, and hors d'oeuvres were in bountiful supply. His wife was there and was very gracious to all the musicians. We parted from the Maestro with a good feeling, although that was certainly not true in many instances with other orchestras.

Reiner returned to the Met in 1962, at a time when we had no prominent conductors for the German repertoire to conduct "Gotterdammerung." Just prior to that, we had done a series of recordings with him for RCA.

Unfortunately during these rehearsals he fell very ill — he had heart disease — and died.

George Szell came to the Metropolitan Opera for the first time in the Fall of 1942, just before I entered the Merchant Marine. I played the preliminary rehearsals for his debut opera, Verdi's "Othello." We, in the orchestra, thought he was a Czech, and were pleased he was not Hungarian, as our

BEHIND THE GOLD CURTAIN

information about Fritz Reiner colored our thinking.

He came to us with a considerable reputation; he had guest conducted for every major symphony and was the permanent conductor of the Cleveland Symphony Orchestra. Szell was an excellent pianist and had an extensive European background as an opera conductor. We soon discovered he was very capable. However, no one is perfect in this life, and that is true of conductors, too.

Szell thought he knew everything better than anyone else. He certainly knew the orchestral score of "Othello," one of the great Verdi operas if not the greatest. Our timpanist, George Brown, was a fine artist — one of the best I had the pleasure of working with in my career. He played in tune and knew the repertoire thoroughly. Szell stopped the orchestra, and informed him that he was not playing the rhythm correctly. Brown had played the opera many times with many other conductors and had had no problems. Szell hounded the poor man, who became Szell's personal victim.

Reiner was known to do the same thing, but was a gentleman with us. Szell was no gentleman. He was sarcastic and arrogant. I had heard of this behavior from musicians who worked with him in Cleveland and from those who had auditioned for him. However, I went into the Service and did not perform further with him.

The Merchant Marine Years

I entered the Merchant Marine in November, 1942. The war was already in progress, and every young man was concerned about his future. We musicians looked to enlist in the most suitable spots for our abilities. Many of us went into Army and Navy bands in Washington. Some found posts out west with newly formed bands. Many musicians entered the Signal Corps, since their training seemed consistent with that.

I was hesitant about where to go, but I knew the longer I waited, the less control I would have over my destiny. I had the opportunity to join the Merchant Marine Band because I knew the conductor of the orchestra, Philip Lang. He was recruiting the best men he could find and that included men from the New York Philharmonic, the NBC Symphony, and the Metropolitan Opera orchestra. The jazz men came from the best bands in the country, Glenn Miller, Benny Goodman, Artie Shaw, and others.

I was the second to join from the Metropolitan Opera orchestra. Eventually, we had a combined band and orchestra of close to a hundred people. I played viola in the orchestra. There were ceremonies every morning on the field to inspire the new recruits. I was twenty-nine years old at this time and in my home city.

The recruits came from all over the country — from farms in the west, from Appalachia, from the south. Most had never left home before or had never seen the ocean. They were frightened and homesick, very ill at ease. The main source of comfort and inspiration to keep up their morale was the Welfare Department of which we were a very important part.

The base was in Sheepshead Bay, Brooklyn; all they had to do to go to the heart of Manhattan was take the subway. Those were the days of the promotion and expansion of USO clubs where civilian performers — especially from the theater — gave these young men some solace and cheer by entertaining them and providing good food at no charge.

We had developed the number one entertainment Welfare Department in greater New York, with our next door neighbr, the Coast Guard. They had people like Jack Dempsey in their sports department, and we had Benny Leoonard. In addition, there were many theatrical personalities, comedians and the like. The leader of the musical division was Jack Lawrence, a famous songwriter of the time. The orchestra had daily rehearsals and we performed at night for the trainees. We played classical and jazz — all kinds of music. When there were dances, the hot jazz men were called to play. Often the strings were included, but often we were excused.

When I entered the Merchant Marine, Roger Moore our trombonist was already in the band. The Chief Petty Officer was Philip Lang. He was bringing new members into the orchestra. I saw immediately that the musicians were excellent and if I had to be in the Service I was very fortunate to be where I was.

Since I was already married, I was permitted to live off-base and come back and forth almost nightly to my home in Forest Hills. I also had gas ration tickets and a half dozen guys in similar circumstances would pile into my car for the trips back and forth.

We were able to lead fairly normal lives outside our obligation to the Service. There were at least ten to twenty-five people in our Metropolitan Opera orchestra due for the draft, so I convinced at least a dozen of them to enlist and just in time.

There was only a month after I had enlisted to enter the Service under the Naval Reserve system, which protected us from draft into the regular Army or Navy. There were no guarantees, and we were under the supervision of the Navy. We always knew there was the possibility that we might be shipped out after our basic training, but the base captain realized we were important to the morale of the trainees, so we were kept at our specialties.

Trainees had a very tough day. In and out of rowboats, studying navigation, sliding and jumping into the water from the ships and rowboats. We all took this arduous basic training.

Some of the members of the Metropolitan orchestra who joined me were Tony Addicicco, tubist; Ozzie Porpora, horn; Martin Leskow, oboe and Steven Maxym, bassoonist. Steve came in too late to be protected by the Naval Reserve and eventually had to go to sea. He was involved in the terrible Bari invasion in Italy.

The unmarried members of the various bands and orchestra lived on base, and they eventually became bored. Many of them did not have to play

BEHIND THE GOLD CURTAIN   55

every night the way the classical musicians did. They were used primarily for the marching bands. (Incidentally, most members of the orchestra were required to play an instrument useful to the marching bands.)

Obviously, string players could not march with fiddles, so most learned to double. I had played saxophone in my college days, but when I found the marching band hard on my embouchure — my lips had become swollen, I had the bright idea of switching to the cymbals. Not a wise choice. I thought it was very clever of me because in the symphony or opera the cymbals are played only a few times in a performance. I had completely overlooked the fact that in a band the cymbals are played at least once every two or four beats. People think it is easy, but it is not. They weigh twenty pounds and get heavier with every step. I should have chosen the triangle!

This marching band routine did not last too long because the brass players — trombone, horns and trumpets — had pistons in their instruments and if the temperature dropped to 30 degrees or below, the pistons would freeze and stick.

None of us were the outdoor type anyhow. We wore our uniforms and bell-bottom trousers with as many sweaters underneath as we could, but our hands were frozen. There was quite a rebellion. The smarter and more experienced members investigated U.S. Navy regulations and discovered that bands were excused from marching on days the temperature dropped below a certain point. However, it took a long time to convince our base captain, who was not a musician but a tie-salesman in civilian life, that there really was such a Navy regulation. When he did not do anything about the matter, we grumbled about the Merchant Marine reversing Navy regulations and eventually we got through to the commander and the marching was eliminated after the first year.

Some of the Met musicians went back in the evening to play performances because there was still a large Wagner repertoire being performed. Leinsdorf was in charge. He had not entered the Service yet, but since most of the men had left, the quality of the performance suffered. A large orchestra was required for these operas, and he tempted them by offering double pay per performance. A few accepted. This was not permitted by the Service.

The pay in the Service was $28 a week for a man living off the base. My apartment rent was $100 a month, so obviously the economics of being in the Service was bad. Everyone thought of somehow augmenting the salary. The Army paid only $22 per month — even worse. Therefore a few took advantage of the Met offer and moonlighted.

Later some members of the orchestra told the Captain of the base and he cautioned us that if any of us were caught moonlighting or making extra money we would be shipped out either on a Merchant Marine vessel, the most dangerous branch of the Service, or to a regular Army or Navy unit. He pointed out that the moonlighters were making more money than he was as Commander.

One or two disregarded this warning, were caught and immediately shipped out. One of our players, the tubist, was sent to upstate New York to a receiving base for the regular Navy, and wrote us of the stringent Navy regulations. He advised us to be grateful for the situation we had and not to jeopardize it.

In the last eight or nine months of the war the regulations were relaxed and we were able to do additional work. The base captain was changed and the assistant commander, a former toothpaste salesman from Detroit, was influential in guiding the Welfare Department; he allowed us to work at night. That's when I followed the lead of many of my colleagues. I was engaged to play in a musical show, contracted by my friend Morris Stonzek, which was housed in the now defunct Ziegfeld Theater at 54th Street and Sixth Avenue in New York. (Flo Ziegfeld had an apartment on the top floor with a viewing booth, so that he could see what went on in the theater at any time.) Billy Rose had purchased this building and produced shows there.

The show I played in was "The Seven Lively Arts." Many of the outstanding performers of the period appeared in it, including the dancers Alicia Markova and Anton Dolin, the Benny Goodman Quintet, the comedians Bert Lahr and Beatrice Lillie. The orchestra was comprised of top people in the profession. I helped bring in a few from the Merchant Marine who were leaders of their sections at the Metropolitan Opera. I would rush home whenever I could get off the base, or drive directly to New York to be ready for an eight o'clock performance, changing from sailor suit to tuxedo for the evening show. This routine lasted for eight months. I had to be on the base by 6:30 AM and I played until midnight. It was a long trip, but in those days there was very little traffic and I could drive very fast.

I also did some moonlighting in a famous radio series — "The Cresta Blanca" program conducted by my dear friend Morton Gould. He invited me to play in the viola section. This was generous of him because he knew my first obligation was to the Merchant Marine, and he could not depend on me. He left the Tuesday night place open for me until three or four hours before the show, with the understanding that if I could not leave the base, I called the contractor so they could arrange a replacement. However, this rarely happened and I managed to play the entire series. All this helped me manage economically. I was finally discharged after three years. It was early fall, 1945, and I rejoined the Metropolitan Opera.

The Metropolitan Opera Orchestra After World War II

After the war, there were many changes at the Metropolitan. New men, for example, were engaged to replace the men who had gone into the Service. And it was very difficult to find certain instrumentalists. Management even hired a Spanish gentleman, a guitarist who played a little viola, to take my place. Of course, he did not last very long; he could not handle the music.

Leonard Grossman auditioned for my job and got it legitimately. He was a fine player. Still, I resented him — resented the fact that he was in my former seat. After all, it was not a law, but it was the common understanding nationwide that servicemen were to return to their previous positions with no loss of seniority.

I appealed to the new personnel manager, an Engishman named John Mundy. He said he could not remove the man. For a period of a few weeks, I fought this with no success. I finally accepted the demotion, which was one stand behind my original place. This was not a matter of ego, but of economics. The further front you were, the more dollars were added to your paycheck. Eventually, I did return to my original seat because of changes in personnel.

Even from my new vantage point, however, I could see that the orchestra, from repertoire to management, had been irrevocably transformed. I would say a good 20 percent of the men had gone off to war. One or two had passed away, and a few had transferred to other positions.

The management and the repertoire had changed considerably because of the war and the anti-German sentiment. When I left the orchestra to enter the Merchant Marine, some 70 percent of the orchestra were foreigners and 30 percent were Americans. Some foreigners, however, returned to their own countries. Others were elderly gentlemen who were at the end of their careers and had retired, and younger players were engaged. The percentage was now reversed.

In the teens and early 1920's, the manager of the Opera house was Gatti-Casazza and his affiliations were with his European colleagues. He had engaged many of the personnel who were there when I entered the Met. Now Edward Johnson was in charge and things had changed completely.

When I came back Rise Stevens had already become a star because of her famous Carmen, Lawrence Tibbett still did some singing, Leonard Warren had won the Metropolitan Auditions of the Air and had become a star — he had been singing at the Met during the three years I had been in the Service. Jan Peerce had been at the Met since 1942. He was engaged to sing operas like "Rigoletto," "La Traviata," lyric tenor roles, and he had a huge following because of his radio work and a world-famous recording of the song, "The Bluebird of Happiness." He had also been a star attraction at Radio City Music Hall for many years. The Met needed him.

One Sunday evening while I was in the Merchant Marine, I was passing the opera house in the company of a fellow serviceman, Fred Buldrini — an excellent violinist. Our paymaster, Amy Gerber, doubled as ticket-taker on the 40th Street side of the house, saw us in uniform and said, "You have to go in to hear a young American tenor named Richard Tucker. I have not heard a voice like this since Caruso." She let us in as standees and this young man appeared to sing his aria for the evening.

It was "Cielo e Mar" from "La Gioconda." This was the most beautiful voice I had heard up to that time as a member of the orchestra. It had everything — vigor, a beautiful quality of sound, everything. This was still during the war so I did not get to know the man until I came back. He was already on the roster and sang both dramatic and lyric roles. Not many singers could do both, and the foreign singers were not available because of the war. By 1945, Rise Stevens had become a big star. She had already sung some very important roles, like Carmen, which made opera history.

A few years after the war Robert Merrill made his entrance. He was a fine baritone, a wonderful addition to the Met roster. Among the women, Licia Albanese, Stella Romano and Zinka Milanov were there. We had a good front line of singers and conductors.

At that time the management brought in Emil Cooper. He was engaged about 1947-1948 and was a valuable addition to the staff as his repertoire included all the Russian operas. He introduced "Kovanchina" to this country. He had also conducted at La Scala and was the basso Chaliapin's favorite conductor.

He was a very short man, snow white hair, quite rotund — he weighed

BEHIND THE GOLD CURTAIN

at least two hundred pounds — and had unusually long arms. When they were stretched out they looked as though they reached from one side of the pit to the other.

He was as solid as rock when he gave a down-beat; contrary to Reiner's style, you could not mistake it. He never tried to speak in Russian to us, just the best English he could. But he had broken delivery of the language. He fractured every word he uttered. He stopped the rehearsal, constantly telling stories trying to prove a point or to tell us of his experiences with Mussorgsky when he conducted "Boris Godunov."

"Boris" had been given at the Met with Chaliapin in the early 30's. I heard him at one of his last concerts. Chaliapin was at the Met during the regime of Arturo Toscanini, who was already world famous from his tenure at La Scala. I had heard this story about them:

At rehearsal, many conductors stress the fact that singers should use full voice so that the orchestra can be properly balanced. But many singers, prima-donnas mostly, insisted on going through the part mezzo-voce. You could not fight them.

Toscanini, however, was not intimidated by anyone, certainly not by singers. Chaliapin came for a rehearsal of "Boris" and excused himself to Toscanini. He said, "Maestro, I am going to talk the part because I do not have much voice today." Toscanini immediately replied, "Mr. Chaliapin, as far as I am concerned you never sing, you always talk your part."

My early experiences with Emil Cooper were fascinating. He was an excellent conductor. I would not put him in a class for certain repertoire with conductors like Panizza and Papi, but these two were no longer available. Papi had died. When he did not arrive for a Saturday afternoon performance and broadcast that Jan Peerce was scheduled to sing, they sent someone to his hotel room and found him on the bathroom floor. He had had a fatal stroke.

Panizza, meanwhile, had returned to Argentina after the war. Cooper was the replacement for these two conductors. Cooper's repertoire included most of the Italian operas, "Louise" of Charpentier, and practically the entire Russian repertoire.

When he rehearsed the orchestra he stopped often to tell a story or to vilify a member of the orchestra. He was very suspicious of everyone and he would attack verbally and venomously.

Many such incidents occurred in my section. We had two or three members who purposely provoked him. Paul Bennett, for example, one of the men who replaced me during the war years, chewed gum all the time and it irritated Cooper to no end. When he caught sight of him he would stop the rehearsal and make a comment in his broken English. It sounded something like this: "Dere is vun viola player in dis section vat is alvays chooing gom and every time I look at him is annoying. I vish he vould stop." Everyone knew immediately it was Paul Bennett. I presume he stopped chewing for a while but he could not get out of the habit. Eventually he left the orchestra in the late 40's.

An elderly gentleman was now sitting at the last stand. He had been at the Met approximately forty years and had paid his dues. Since he was a tall angular man, and had long arms, he had been holding the viola up for many years, and he had a habit of extending his arm and resting the viola down towards his lap.

Conductors, especially Cooper, became suspicious if the violins and the violas were not held up or if a trumpet or trombone were not held up to the lips. He wanted everyone to look energetic and keep his head and instrument up in the air. Again he said in his broken English, "Dere is vun viola player vat alvays plays mit his viola on his stomach." He would then say, "You should please stop it."

At that time it was still possible for a conductor to fire you. He could not fire you on the spot unless you ridiculed him or were not doing your job, but at the end of the season he could insist that your contract not be renewed. So these remarks were very funny but they were very serious to the people involved. We were in jeopardy.

The conductors were our sole bosses and at the end of the season they were the ones who determined who stayed and who left. It was the same with the chorus. During the rest of the rehearsal, he constantly looked in our direction. I suppose he wanted to see if the comment or the warning looks had any effect on the guilty man. Well, when he looked at the victim of his comment, I thought he was looking at me; my stand partner at the time, Godfrey Laefsky, thought he was looking at him, and we were both whispering to one another, "Who does he mean? You or me?" When intermission came we discussed it and decided to confront him.

Neither of us was guilty. We were both young men and played with our instruments high in the air. I am sure we showed a great deal more enthusiasm and energy than many of the other members of the orchestra, especially poor old Peyre. When we approached him we asked, "Maestro, when you made that comment were you looking at either one of us?" He put his arms on our shoulders and had a little grin on his face and the comment he made was, "Aha! So you both hev ah guilty conscience!" But he added, "No, it vas not you." We went back to our seats greatly relieved although it was a disturbing incident to us because our jobs were at stake.

Now a story about Cooper and me, which affected my own life. I had two very young children in 1946-47 and I did not get much sleep in those days; after all, there I was with two children crying all night and working at the Met all day. We were rehearsing "La Gioconda" and it is quite a long opera — close to four hours. The first acts are close to an hour long. The third act is the famous ballet "Dance of the Hours" and the fourth act is quite long.

Cooper was renowned for long rehearsals. In those days they did not have the limitations we have today. A rehearsal would start and after three hours or four hours it would be three or four in the afternoon. We were all tired except for Cooper. He went over passages. He never got tired. We referred to spots to go back to by numbers on the parts, and each part had the same number after so many measures. The number Cooper returned to was #308. He went back to this number at least twenty times. It got to a point, after the eighth or ninth time, that whenever he stopped the orchestra, the players automatically shouted, "#308! 308! 308!"

Gunther Schüller, noted today as a conductor and composer, played French horn in the orchestra then. He knew Cooper was an avid White Russian — anti-Communist — and Schüller wore something red every day, a shirt, or a tie, to taunt Cooper. However, Cooper did not dare mess around with the horn players because he was afraid they would sabotage his performances, so he always picked on the weaker members.

When we were in our fifth hour of rehearsal, we had not reached the fourth act. We were playing "Dance of the Hours."

One of the other horn players, David Rattner, was sitting next to me. At one spot neither of us had anything to do, so we had an opportunity to chat. At another spot neither one of us had to play so he said to me, "You know when I played at Radio City Music Hall, this famous solo spot," and he sang the melody that the cellos were playing, "we used to play it on the French horn." He explained that, in the Erno Rapee days at the Music Hall, one instrument would take another's part if they did not have the right number of instruments for the score. I was being distracted and I was sleepy and tired. In that part during the "Dance of the Hours" there is a ten-measure rest for viola in the final part of the dance, which is a fast two count — the orchestra comes to life. The rhythm is very precise; the brass comes in there and it is loud.

I had a silver-tipped bow and unconsciously tapped the time on the stand. The stands were made of metal and the sound was like castanets and then it was time for me to join in. By the time I put the bow on the string to play with the section, Cooper had waved his long arms to stop the orchestra. He looked in my direction, pointed at me as though he was going to put a sword through my heart, and shouted, "You! For vy you make dot doity noise?" This was a dress rehearsal with a full house audience. If there had been a trap door, I would have gone through it.

He hesitated a moment and I had no comment as he had caught me in the act. Again, "For vy you make dot doity noise? Come to my room after the act." After the dance in another four or five minutes, the act had ended. I was trembling and prepared to go to the conductor's room. Our first violist, a good friend, John DiJanni, said, "Look, Dave, do you want me to go with you? Cooper is very fond of me. He speaks Italian and I speak Italian. Maybe we can settle this thing." I said, "John, what can you do for me? He caught me. I have no defense."

We both fully expected I would be fired on the spot. I went to his room, and found him pacing back and forth, hands in his pockets. The room was very small so as soon as he came to one wall he turned around and started to pace to the other. I just waited. He had sent for the manager of the orchestra, John Mundy, and he wanted Edward Johnson, the general manager, to come. It was obvious he was going to fire me. So when he asked me again, "For vy you make dat doity noise?" I said, "Maestro. I did not intend to offend you. We had five hours of rehearsals. My mind was wandering and I instinctively kept the rhythm with my bow and I had a bad night."

The excuse I made did not make too much sense to him. Finally, the general manager had arrived and I said, "Maestro, if I wanted to annoy you or offend you I would have gone back to the tympani section, picked up some mallets and really made a sound you could not mistake! I was just waiting to come in. I had a rest period."

He looked at me and said, "You mean it? You did not try to annoy me?" He patted me on the back and said, "All right, good boy, go back and ve vill finish the opera."

From that day on, I knew he never trusted me. All conductors are paranoid; they are always suspicious. He always kept one eye on me and believe me, it taught me a lesson.

The rehearsals for "Boris Godunov" were a unique experience under Emil Cooper. We had given "Boris" before with Panizza conducting during Pinza's hey day. The first time with Cooper, who was Russian, came in the late 40's. The orchestra parts were awful. They looked as though they were hand written, barely legible. I do not recall if we played the Shostakowitch version or Mussorgsky's original score.

We had gone through the opera after the first rehearsal and the maestro stopped the orchestra to tell us tales of his past experiences with the opera.

BEHIND THE GOLD CURTAIN

Some conductors show a great deal of confidence and trust in the orchestra and others feel that they have to teach the orchestra right from the beginning. He spoke to us as though we had never played the opera, which was not true. It was a lengthy speech in which he explained the opera's construction. We went through most of the operas we performed from beginning to end. They were always in the repertoire as they were very popular. Not so with "Boris Godunov." So in Cooper's first lengthy speech to the orchestra, he said in his broken English, "Gentlemen, I vant you all to know that I conducted in 1900 'Boris' in Russia, vit such singers as Chaliapin and many other prominent singers, so I know this opera probably as well as any man in de vorld."

He proceeded to instruct us further. "Dis is an opera put togedder from ten different little pieces and ve must connect all de pieces togedder. So you must vatch me very closely and listen to me. Please gentlemen, take home the parts and overlook."

Another one of his favorite statements was, "Also please gentlemen, do not come too yearly." This meant "do not come too soon" in playing, not arrival.

He had many idiosyncrasies in manner and language. He had his favorites who could do no wrong and thought him very amazing. Though he was not a great conductor, he had great integrity as an artist. He felt it was his job to round us out and make us a unit—one body of men. He knew from experience that an orchestra consists of many different temperaments and it was his job—I cannoot say he was wrong—to unite us as a body. He wanted to get a good performance especially with an opera like "Boris Godunov." We accepted this with an opera like "Boris" as he probably had much experience conducting this score. Later as I played the opera with other conductors, I realized that others did it just as well and in some ways even better.

Cooper was caught up in the conductor's syndrome: He could do no wrong and he could be ruthless. I would not classify him as a great gentleman; he was not considerate of anyone's feeling except his own.

I recall some incidents vividly. We were performing either "Gioconda" or "Aida." The Met had engaged a new singer from Yugoslavia. She was of medium height, stout, with a very interesting face. From the few operas she sang, other than those conducted by Emil Cooper, she proved to be very competent. However, the relationship between Cooper and Mme. Ilyitch, whatever it was, indicated that Emil Cooper was not fond of her and he made her life miserable at the Met. He would not follow her, he would drown her out, he would do nothing a conscientious conductor should have done to help a singer, and God knows the singers need all the help they can get. As a result her career at the Met was short-lived.

He treated many other singers in the same manner. When a conductor does not cooperate with a singer, it can actually end a career. And if Cooper did not like you, he not only made life miserable, he set out to destroy you. A new singer had the problem of adapting to the house. As I mentioned previously the Met is enormous and it takes a while to get used to. None of this behavior on Cooper's part helped the performance.

We in the orchestra were well aware of all this and I was discussing this with a colleague, the contralto Regina Resnik. She said, "I never had this problem with Emil Cooper! Our relationship was always fine. As a matter of fact it was too fine. We shared a car on one occasion and were discussing the pros and cons of opera and before I knew it this fat little man had his hand on my knee and the subject changed abruptly. I was well aware that his hand was traveling. Of course, I had to do what was necessary to stop this." He would accompany a singer very well if he liked her or wanted to seduce her.

One final tale about this colorful conductor. He was engaged to conduct "Fidelio" of Beethoven at a summer opera series, in Central City, Colorado, a little mining town some forty miles north of Denver where I played for ten summers as first violist. The town is 10,000 feet high, two miles high, and the atmosphere is rarefied. It takes some people months to adjust. Some cannot live there at all. Bloody noses, palpitations, fainting — all these symptoms manifest themselves with exertion.

The year was 1952. We were rehearsing the "Leonore" overture to "Fedelio," a work that requires much activity on the part of the conductor. We were half-way through when suddenly Cooper collapsed. He was bleeding from the nose, white as a sheet, and lay prone on the floor unconscious. We were positive he had had a heart attack. After all he was in his 60's.

A doctor was summoned immediately, and he examined him and announced to everyone that Maestro Cooper had no heart attack, merely an attack of altitude sickness. He came to and the doctor advised him to take it easy for a few days until he had adjusted to the altitude. He listened to the diagnosis and advice, stood up and asked, "You mean I didn't hev a heart attack?" The doctor repeated his diagnosis. So Cooper mounted the podium, stretched out his ape-like arms and said, "Okay, ladies and gentlemen, let's start from the beginning," and he proceeded to finish the rehearsal.

Jerome Hines came to the Met in 1947-48. He was a young basso, tall (six foot four or taller), slim, good looking, a graduate of a California institute of metaphysics, as I recall, so his studies as a singer started rather late.

I met him in California while we were on tour. He was in "Don Giovanni." The circumstances that precipitated our meeting were as follows: When we played in Los Angeles, we used an arena, some 6,000 to 8,000 seats all on one level. It was built for athletic events, certainly not for opera, but that is where we performed.

A young lady in the front row leaned towards me and asked if I could arrange a meeting with Jerome Hines as she had personal regards from people he knew. I said I would try. At the end of the second performance, I escorted the young lady to his dressing room. I knew Jerome Hines casually, but I never had any particular reason to discuss anything with him. I knocked on his door and brought this young lady with me. She was a student and very attractive. I introduced her to Jerome Hines, telling him the circumstances of my meeting with her. (She attended every performance he sang.)

He was sitting at his dressing table, doing his make-up. He was very fastidious about his make-up — he did not trust anyone to do it and the role of "Don Giovanni" required a great deal of make-up (sideburns, goatee, etc.). I introduced them and, much to our surprise, she suggested poiners to him on how to make-up. Originally, I thought he would act kindly towards this young girl since she was so attractive. Instead, because of the unsolicited advice she gave, he turned on her with indignation and said, "Look, I do not need anyone like you telling me about my make-up. I consider myself an artist when it comes to that." The visit ended abruptly.

Still, I was one of Jerome Hines's most ardent boosters and we soon became friends. I was very much impressed with him when he was featured in a then new opera by Benjamin Britten, "Peter Grimes." It was commissioned by the Koussevitzky Foundation and the Metropolitan had made quite a production of it. It was the talk of the town and considered the greatest modern opera. Today, it is a part of the standard opera repertory, though many people just do not understand it and some do not like it.

Hines also sang parts like Sparafucile in "Rigoletto," the Grand Inquisitor in "Don Carlo" and more. When Rudolf Bing became general manager in 1950, the first opera under his administration was "Don Carlo" on the opening night of the season. He imported an entirely new cast, including the mezzo-soprano Fedora Barbieri, a soprano from South America, and Caesare Siepi the basso. He was a young Italian basso who had a great reputation in Europe. I think he was about twenty-eight. Bing was responsible for his debut at the Metropolitan Opera, and he was an instantaneous success. Unfortunately, I would say he presented competition for Hines, who was just coming up as a promising American star. Bing was very proud of his importations and most of them were Italian, French or German. So Siepi stole some of the thunder from Jerome Hines. Instead of singing more roles, he had fewer opportunities to sing.

Jerome Hines still went on to become one of the best singers on the roster. He knew his own worth, as when he sang Boris in "Boris Godunov." Hines, Siepi, and in his short term at the Met, George London, all did the same version in the 50's that Fritz Stiedry conducted, an arrangement by Karl Rathaus. The death scene was a spectacle to behold, when Boris topples down an eight-foot flight of stairs. One basso tried to outdo the other. But they all put on a stellar performance.

In the 70's, my daughter, Phebe Berkowitz, the former Executive Stage Director at the Metropolitan Opera, directed "Boris Godunov" and told me just how special it was working with Jerome Hines as he was a fine artist and a great actor.

His career expanded in other directions, too. He wrote a religious opera and has presented it all over the world. He is highly respected in the artistic community by everyone.

It was a coincidence that started my friendship with Giuseppe DiStefano, the great Italian tenor. When he came to the United States — I would say he made his debut about the same time as Jerome Hines — he sang operas such as "Rigoletto," "Tales of Hoffman," "Faust," many of the lyric operas, and also "Manon" by Massenet. I never got a good look at him unless I clandestinely stood up to peek at the stage. He was in costume, and I could see he was very handsome, but I had no idea of how he looked in street clothes. When the rehearsals were over or the operas were finished, the musicians and chorus headed for the exits as quickly as possible. We did not linger and we never had occasion to speak with the singers until later on. I had no idea of DiStefano's appearance off-stage until we went on our first transcontinental tour.

Our wig maker, a man in his late 70's, was Eddie Senz; we called him "Pop" Senz. He had been with the Met thirty or forty years. Wig-making was entirely different then. One man did all the work with the help of a few assistants. All the work was done by "Pop" Senz personally, and he made sure that all wigs were properly fitted. "Pop" Senz was in close contact with all the singers, and all the singers felt he was one of the most important members of the organization. They told him about their personal problems, and often asked him to help solve them.

He came to me on this tour and said, "Look, David, young DiStefano would like to get an American driver's license. He knows how to drive a car, but he needs a car to take the test. Do you think you can help, and come along to the License Bureau with us?" I said I would be glad to help, but that I did not have a car. In those days you could not rent one easily, there was no Hertz or Avis. I called a cousin of mine with whom I was visiting during our two-week stay in Los Angeles on tour and told him the circumstances. He had a red convertible, and said he would be happy to lend us the car. "However," he said, "I'll have to drive the car to the License Bureau in Beverly Hills as you don't have a California license."

I arranged with my cousin — his name was Grishman — he later became a well-known movie producer, but at that time he was a very young man and was interested in anyone connected with the arts — to get the car and pick up "Pop" Senz, DiStefano, and I at the hotel to drive to the Beverly Hills License Bureau. "Pop" Senz introduced me to DiStefano. I had no idea he was so youthful and handsome. He had jet black hair combed back, and he looked just like a young Rudolf Valentino — the face, the burning eyes. He was full of energy, his eyes dashing in every direction, especially when he saw or smelled a skirt a mile away.

He recognized immediately that I was a fan of his, and I in turn made up my mind to help him out in any way I could. We drove to the License Bureau. It was an imposing building set in the heart of Beverly Hills and resembled a country club more than it did a License Bureau. We parked the car, and came into this huge place to get the proper instruction for obtaining a license. As soon as we entered the building, DiStefano began to sing so that everyone knew there was either a star of the opera or a crackpot in the building.

He had to take a written test consisting of twenty questions about his knowledge of traffic regulations. We were informed by the clerk that the test was given in Spanish or English. DiStefano had been in the country only a short time. He certainly could not speak English, and I doubt he could write in Spanish. He asked if he could take the test orally and the clerk agreed. He misunderstood all twenty questions and answered "Si" instead of "No" and "No" instead of "Si." Every answer was wrong! However, they proceeded to give him the actual driving test. As luck would have it the inspector was an opera lover, and had heard him sing at the performance the previous evening. He took him out for a mile or so to test him about turns, hand signals, and parking — there were no automatic signals then.

DiStefano had told us he could drive a car, but what happened during the examination, the test itself, we did not know. When he pulled up at the bottom of the marble stairs in front of the building, we who were at the top of the stairs — "Pop" Senz, my cousin, and myself — were eagerly awaiting the decision of the inspector.

At the time, in California, you received an instantaneous license if you passed the test. We saw the inspector lecturing him about putting out his hand when making a left turn — he was showing him how to do it. Apparently he had messed up. We took bets that he did not pass. When they arrived at the top of the stairs to where we were waiting to do the necessary paper work, the inspector addressed us and said, "Gentlemen, I am happy to announce that I have the great privilege of giving Mr. DiStefano his first American driving license," and he issued the license on the spot.

DiStefano asked my cousin if he could drive us all back to the hotel now that he had his license. He wanted to take us all out for coffee. As we were looking for a coffee shop, my cousin noticed that DiStefano was driving with his head in every direction — not necessarily the direction we were traveling. Every time he saw a pretty girl he forgot to look straight ahead. My cousin, the car's owner, was not too happy so he said, "Look, you better let me drive the car home."

Later, I heard that DiStefano was engaged to sing in Mexico City the following summer, and his driving was so careless he reportedly had a number of accidents.

As a singer, however, he became a huge success. He always upstaged the soprano, particularly if she was not to his taste. If she was a woman of considerable size, or one who did not appeal to him, or would not date him, he would come to the edge of the stage, look down into the orchestra pit and, since we were quite friendly, he would wink at me and indicate in gesture that he wanted to throw the soprano into the pit. Even while singing he was a clown. He was very sure of himself and was well aware that he was a great favorite of the public.

When Bing came to the Met, there were difficulties about DiStefano's on-stage behavior, and probably about money as well. He left for his native Italy, and became a star there in dramatic tenor roles. He himself told me that an Italian impresario had approached him to sing roles like "La Forza del Destino" and that if the impresario would give him time to learn the role, plus a handsome bonus, he would do it. He learned "La Forza" in a week and was given an outboard motor boat and jewelry in addition to a generous fee. He told me he was a hero in Italy, just like a baseball star in the United States.

In 1953 or 1954 Bing sent for him to return to the Met, and there was great difficulty with the negotiations regarding his contract. He was already a bigger star in Europe than he had ever been in the United States. He wanted certain considerations and allowances for his family and Bing refused to grant his wishes.

DiStefano finally did accept Bing's conditions for his return to the Metropolitan; one of them was that he was not permitted to sing anything but lyric roles, just as he had previously at the Met. His voice had already changed. Instead of waiting for the voice to become dramatic in timbre, he forced his voice into a heavier sound and it did considerable damage. The people in the opera house who were particularly interested in his career, especially the Italians who knew I was his friend, were dismayed. One violinist in particular, Vico, the Assistant Concertmaster, would look across the orchestra pit at me and shake his head slightly as though to say, "His voice isn't the same."

One day DiStefano asked me to come to his dressing room. He wanted to know the impression of the orchestra men about his voice. Naturally, I was forced to lit a bit and say, "Oh they still think you're great." Unfortunately, it was not true. He did not remain too many more years and went back to Italy. He stretched his career out long after its normal course. In the 60's he performed a series of recitals with Maria Callas and although I did not hear him then, I understand the voice was finished. He had an interesting but short-lived career.

When I returned to the Metropolitan Opera in 1945 after my military service, Richard Tucker was already on the roster and singing leading dramatic roles. He began to share many of the tenor roles with the other singers in the organization. The more I heard him sing, the more impressed I was. He was just beginning leading roles and his repertoire was increasing constantly.

I later found he was a very friendly man, democratic with his colleagues, and we started a friendship that lasted some thirty years until his too-early demise. I remember vividly the first transcontinental tour we made in 1947-48, the first after the war. When we landed in the western part of the country, in Los Angeles, we had many occasions to dine together and discuss the opera. He was always in awe at some of his colleagues, and always gave due credit to other artists, even tenors who were his competition. There was one exception — his brother-in-law, Jan Peerce, his wife Sarah's, brother.

Sarah and Richard were a very devoted couple, and were always together. Sarah had a great deal to do with furthering Richard's career because she was always supportive. He started out as a salesman in the textile industry and became a very successful button salesman for the fur industry. But when he began to sing and found he had a good voice, he studied cantorial singing. He became the outstanding cantor in the city and had his choice of any position.

I discovered he had sung in his early years for a synagogue in the Bronx; the Rabbi who had worked with him at that time told me about it. Later he joined the most important temple in Brooklyn on Eastern Parkway where he sang his last public engagements as a cantor, except for those times he was invited to the Hotel Concord in Upper New York State for the High Holy Days. He was the highest paid cantor for those three days, two days of Rosh Hashanah and one of Yom Kippur. He was religious though not fanatically so, as he sang at the opera on all Jewish holidays except for the High Holy Days.

Getting back to the early operatic years, the conversation that struck me with a great deal of interest was how he viewed some of the singers at the opera. He spoke highly of Zinka Milanov, who was his partner in most of his operas, and of one particular performance that another important singer, Kurt Baum, a tenor, sang of "Aida." Baum was from Germany and had been trained there. Many members of the orchestra were not too impressed with him. However, he had a high "C" that came out like a bomb blast, and when he sang "Celeste Aida," which is the important aria for tenor in the opera, he did not spare himself. He had three more hours to go in the opera and he sang it with such enthusiasm, strength, and power, whether you liked the quality of the voice or not, you had to admire the man's ability, and you certainly heard him.

When Tucker discussed it with me the day after the performance, he said, "There is only one Radames in this world, and that's Kurt Baum." I was surprised to hear him speak so generously of his colleague, especially another tenor. Tucker was always careful of his voice and he felt at that time it was too soon for him to sing the role of Radames, as it puts a tremendous strain on the voice.

His relationship with his brother-in-law, Jan Peerce, was not good. Although we all knew they did not get along at all, no one ever found out the reason for this estrangement. Jan Peerce had joined the Met some three or four years before Tucker and was a top-notch singer. He had a beautiful voice, especially for the roles he sang at the Met, the lyric roles. He would have loved to sing more dramatic roles such as Don Jose in "Carmen," but the management was careful to give him roles like "Rigoletto," "Traviata," and "Boheme." He had no real competition in those roles and when Tucker came along and began to sing the more dramatic roles such as "La Gioconda" and also sang the same roles that Jan Peerce sang, some people thought it was the competition that created the breach. I think, however, that it was more family strain than anything else. Tucker often spoke to me in a deprecating manner about his brother-in-law. He once said, "He appears to the world as such a pious man." Peerce was not a cantor although he knew the singing. The father of Sarah and Jan had been an important member in the Lower East Side Temple, but when the father retired, he went to live with Richard Tucker, not his son. Sarah Tucker kept a kosher home all her life and perhaps that was one reason.

Jan Peerce had been established for a considerably longer period than Richard Tucker. He had made a lot of money from the Radio City Music Hall, and from a national broadcast on Sunday morning. He had recorded a song "The Bluebird of Happiness" that was a hit and produced substantial royalties for many years.

Richard Tucker implied that his brother-in-law was a bit of a hypocrite. He said, "His father is living with me. I'm supporting him instead of his son." There must have been some personal conflict about that issue. Then he brought up the point that despite the fact that Jan Peerce was deeply religious — it was known to all that Peerce prayed every morning according to Jewish ritual with phylacteries and never ate anything but kosher food — he did sing on Saturday, the Hebrew Sabbath. Tucker said further, "Here is his son, brought up in so orthodox a manner, yet he married a gentile, out of the faith." I thought this a foolish comment but I held my tongue.

Jan's son, Larry, later became a very successful film producer.

When we were working in Puerto Rico on a private engagement, we had attended the opera season there. Tucker said, "Let's all go out for something to eat after the performance, Davey Boy." He always called me that, but earlier before he remembered my name, he used to call me, "Harry." The group consisted of Peerce, his wife, the Tuckers, and my wife and myself. Tucker was about my age, give or take a few months. Then he said, "I'm the only tenor in the world that would offer my brother-in-law, under the circumstances, a free cup of coffee, and he would accept it!" There was a very obvious enmity.

Jan Peerce, with whom I had occasion to spend some time on tour, never brought up the relationship. I do not think he knew that Tucker and I were such close friends.

One day about the same period, I spent the afternoon with Jan in St. Louis, Missouri. He met me on the street, and said, "Why don't you come shopping with me? I'm looking for some ties." I asked him why he needed me for that and he said, "I'm color-blind and you can help me."

We went to one of the department stores there, I think it was Baer, Stix and Fuller, this was in the late 50's. We went to the tie counter and he bought half a dozen silk ties, paid the listed price and then we parted. As soon as

I left him, I left the main floor, went to the bargain basement where they sold the same merchandise at a third of the price, and I bought myself a half dozen ties. He never discovered my savings.

As time passed my friendship with Richard Tucker developed more and more. Whenever we had occasion to speak with each other over the years he would bring me up to date on the progress of his career, and his family. His career was progressing in leaps and bounds, and he was very proud of the fact that his competence was being recognized by the public and his colleagues. One of the things I respected about Richard Tucker was that every time he sang he gave one hundred percent of himself during rehearsal or performance. He always sang full voice, sang to the best of his ability, and with great enthusiasm. Some people criticized his acting, but it was impressive from my point of view, and of course, his voice was one of the greatest for the roles he sang.

He often told me about his engagements and financial successes, about his future plans, about a concert he was going to do, or a concert he had done, and how successful he was as a cantor, and the tremendous fees he commanded. I was very impressed, as my salary at the Metropolitan was not very impressive at that point in the 50's. He augmented his Met salary considerably with his outside duties. When Rudolf Bing came to the Met in that same period, Tucker became his favorite tenor and he gave him every consideration he possibly could.

One summer when I was playing first viola at the summer opera season in Central City, Colorado, Richard Tucker decided to take his family to a dude ranch in Estes Park, Colorado, a national park ninety miles north of Central City. He came to the performance one night and, after that, we all went to the Teller House in Central City, a little bar where singers congregated and entertained informally. They were young singers who were paid with a beer or a sandwich. They enjoyed performing, and the opera patrons were delighted. Tucker was present that evening and, of course, the singers were honored by his presence and sang their hearts out for him. He was with Sarah, of course, and he insisted my family come to Estes Park to visit him at the ranch for a picnic. He also invited our first horn player David Rattner and his wife. It was in 1954 or 55. We all set out on this expedition in two cars. My wife, my three children, and Mr. and Mrs. Rattner.

We arrived at this dude ranch, had our picnic and a pleasant afternoon. It was dinner time, and Tucker insisted we stay for a huge barbecue the owner of the ranch was preparing. He had a half dozen grills going, steak and corn and all the trimmings. The fee was $5 a person, which meant a $25 fee for me, a considerable sum in those days. When it came to paying my fee Tucker put his hand on my hand and said, "Davey Boy, you're not paying for this!" I took my hand out of my pocket immediately and I said, "I brought my whole family here. I don't expect to be your guest for dinner as well as our picnic." "Don't be foolish. In case you don't know it, I sang in Grant Park in Chicago two weeks ago. I sang three numbers and they paid me the astounding fee of $10,000."

In those days it was the equivalent of $50,000; today, perhaps even more. That was the first of many occasions we spent with Richard and Sarah, and their three sons, Barry, David, who later became a noted physician, and the youngest who is now an attorney. Barry is in finance, and is the director of the Richard Tucker Foundation. After this outing, the Tuckers continued their journey out west, and we all returned to the Met after the summer.

Labor Relations at the Met

There is an old expression, "An army marches on its stomach"; this held true for us, too, and throughout the music world generally. Musicians in 1936 were looked upon in a very different light than they are today. In Europe, we were considered "gypsies"; in the United States we were held in low esteem. However, as music appreciation grew via the media of radio and television, people began to look upon the average good musician as an artist, and in a class with other professionals such as doctors, lawyers and teachers.

When I began in opera, money was not the great objective. It was, after all, at the depth of the Great Depression and everyone was happy to get a job, any job, especially with such an esteemed organization as the Metropolitan Opera Association. The same applied to the New York Philharmonic Symphony.

We were paid enough to survive on. We were able to live more comfortably than an average civil service worker, so we continued along those lines, without making undue demands until after the war when inflation began to set in.

Most unions and their leaders saw to it that the conditions of the rank and file gradually improved. Unfortunately, we were at the back of the pack. The average employed musician did rather well in New York — better than a school teacher or a police officer, for example. But in the late 40's, we began to realize that we were choking to death. Rents went up, prices went up, there were no longer those sales where you could buy a good man's shirt for a dollar. Prices were constantly going up for everything.

We began to scream and holler, but we realized we had very little support for our complaints. The musician's union, Local 802 in New York, was very ineffective and weak. The officers of the union were not paid very much and they were glad to have a job. They certainly would not go to bat for the rank and file, as they were afraid of jeopardizing their own status. It was like pulling teeth to rouse them to action when we told them we must have better working conditions and needed more money to survive.

In the late 40's — around 1948 or 1949 — I experienced my first strike to improve our working conditions. The opposition from management was very strong. And with our limited experience we were afraid to move forward in any direction. The result was a strike conducted in a very haphazard manner.

The season was about to start on a Monday. We stated we would not come back to start it unless some concessions were made. I was on the orchestra committee and we met at union headquarters. Our union officers haggled half-heartedly with management, and the strike was settled on Saturday or Sunday. As a member of the orchestra committee, I joined the union officers in making telephone calls to each member to report on Monday. We did not have to pay for the phone calls from union headquarters, and that in itself was a concession. We managed to get going with minimal increases.

The Bing Era began when Rudolf Bing took over the management from Edward Johnson and became General Manager and Director. We soon discovered his thinking regarding the Metropolitan Opera. He wished to enhance its importance in the eyes of the world, and in his own way.

His priority was the visual approach to opera. We already had a weekly radio broadcast so that the public could hear opera. Bing introduced many new productions, and managed to get subscribers, wealthy patrons, to pay for them. Many contributors specified how the money was to be spent: for the benefit of the production itself and not for the benefit of the working people of the Met. This was a sad state of affairs. We did not know how to combat it. Nevertheless, that was the situation, and inflation was rising higher daily.

At that time, I had need for larger living quarters and every time I looked for something, my comment was, "Impossible! I can't afford it." When I returned to look the next year, the price was another 20 percent higher. I realized that something had to be done to maintain a decent standard of living and support a growing family.

I must reiterate that to me the opera was always the most exciting employment one could wish for. There was never a day without a dramatic experience. No fiction or actual occurrence could duplicate the excitement of the opera as compared to the symphony. There was always an outburst — a temperamental fit by a singer in a variety of languages, there was always a conductor who pulled his hair out, or smashed a watch or broke his baton out of frustration. There was intrigue at the opera on and off the stage, just as in a royal palace; and there was always the General Manager, Mr. Bing, who would harass us when we came to him for some special consideration such as an extra night off to attend family functions of any kind. He was always very sarcastic and said, "Gentlemen, I suppose you would just like us to mail you the check each week instead of coming to pick it up, let alone play the operas." Such an attitude was belittling.

We soon learned that the opera comprised fourteen unions. Of these, the orchestra was usually the leader in trying to improve working conditions. Although it was not in writing, the house did practice the system whereby, if it was determined there was an increase in the budget for the orchestra, they would necessarily have to add that percentage to the rest of the house. We could understand that, being a non-profit organization and not having unlimited funds, it was a problem for them. But, we, the younger members of the orchestra, the Americans in the opera house, began to wake up to the fact that we were living in a modern-day world and we could not, as they did previously, save a few dollars and go back to Italy or France, or wherever, and live at a third of the cost of living in the United States.

As always, the executives took care of themselves first. They had the advantage of augmenting their incomes through private enterprise. They had teaching connections, lectures, and worked with agents in Europe who split fees. But we remained at a constant level and something had to be done about it. Medical costs and rents were going sky-high and we had no benefits at all. We had no instrument insurance, no health benefits, and we certainly had no pension or unemployment benefits.

Since we were employed by a non-profit organization we were considered self-employed just like other professionals, like doctors and lawyers. Therefore we did not qualify for Social Security until the law was changed in 1952. Benefits were started only when they were incorporated into our contracts in the early 50's. I was involved in the fight for benefits to a great extent as I had some financial background in the insurance business, and I could see what was happening.

I took insurance courses in 1949 and received a license to work for the Equitable Life Assurance Society; this saved my skin in the early 50's. I received some health benefits from them and was able to augment my income so that I could handle my finances a little better. Several musicians dabbled in other fields. One colleague and his wife imported jewelry and did rather well. Others made reeds for woodwind instruments to sell to other musicians around the country. One or two dabbled in real estate. The majority, however, were not equipped to do anything else, especially if they had little formal education or a poor command of the English language. One or two foreign musicians were knowledgeable about art and had the foresight to purchase master drawings in Europe and amass fine collections.

It was in the 50's that a series of strikes forced Mr. Bing to realize that something had to be done. Mr. Bing was only concerned with the beauty of the stage. His contempt for the musicians and other workers at the opera was well-known, and it did not endear him to any of us.

I admit that everything combined — the stage, the publicity, the famous singers — did enhance the production of opera to make it what it is today, spectacular and big-business, albeit non-profit. But the financial condition of the opera in the 50's was not good. Management had to struggle with replacing singers, which is an on-going problem, as singers come and go, and it was necessary to bring in famous artists to attract patrons. This was the era of Callas, Tebaldi, DelMonaco, Siepi, Barbieri, and these singers had important careers in Europe and demanded huge fees. Opera in Europe was subsidized and opera people were looked upon as nobility.

This was all fine, but we still had to pay our rent. By 1952 we had doubled the length of our season from twelve weeks in 1936 to twenty-six weeks. The exception was 1948 and 1949 when ten weeks were added because we made transcontinental tours.

We still had none of the benefits that were necessary to live decently. In the early 50's I brought in some financial experts to speak to the orchestra, trying to convince them to organize their own health plan. Nothing was done about it because it was an added expense, and no-one could afford the premiums! The committee called a meeting at my insistence about instrument insurance, and we hired a private broker and paid it ourselves. We had no hospitalization, and no pension, however.

There was a system called "severance pay," which meant that for each year we were there, a certain percentage of our salary would be allocated to us in a lump sum settlement if we were not re-engaged. The amounts, however, were negligible.

Gradually, in the middle 50's, we began to make headway in improving our financial situation. In 1955 or 1956 the opera granted Blue Cross, which was paid for by management. We also had the benefit of unemployment insurance from New York State since we were now covered by Social Security. The rate was $25 per week, but it managed to cover a period of a half year. The system was so efficient in New York City that in many boroughs only those who were able to prove they had no other income were able to collect that insufficient amount.

The first time I applied for unemployment benefits in Jamaica, Long Island, I waited in line almost four hours for my turn. A gentleman standing next to me was elegantly dressed — white flannel trousers and dark blue jacket. He said that he owned two boats and lots of real estate, but he had no income as a worker, and could collect unemployment insurance as this was the primary criterion for eligibility. He told me he had been collecting for years, so this made me confident I would qualify. When I filled out the form and was interviewed, I naively acknowledged I was working as an insurance agent. I was immediately disqualified. I fought the case briefly by explaining that though I was listed as an agent, I did not have any income unless I sold insurance, and I needed help. I lost the case, and I was never able to collect unemployment benefits.

We had tried to emulate the New York Philharmonic Symphony, which gave pension fund benefit concerts for its members, with the cooperation of conductors, soloists and management. Management prohibited us from doing so, though in the late 40's we did convince management to let us give a pension concert for the orchestra only (excluding the ballet and chorus).

Most of the workers at the Metropolitan Opera participated, about five hundred in all. I do not recall how much was raised but this money was supposed to start some kind of pension fund because nothing was being done by management. To this day I do not know what happened to that money. The issue was brought up many times, but the funds were never distributed, and management charged it was lost or buried. It may still be in existence; of course, it would not amount to much today. And most of the workers it would have benefited have either left or died.

In the absence of a pension fund, our only hope was an increase in severance pay which, if lucky, we could turn into a real pension. The pension was not to become a reality until many years later — in the early 60's.

The author, David Berkowitz, at 18 years of age.

David Berkowitz at 70, prior to retirement from the Metropolitan Opera Orchestra

Dolores Soyer, Editor/Collaborator

Heldentenor Lauritz Melchior

James Levine, Artistic Director & Principle Conductor
photo by Jorg Reichardt

Dimitri Mitropoulos conducting the Met Orchestra

Soloist Rise Stevens

Conductor Artur Bodanzky

Conductor Edward Johnson looking out over the old Met.

Tenor Richard Tucker

Composer/Conductor Morton Gould

Conductor Fausto Cleva

Conductor Erich Leinsdorf

Viola section of the Met Orchestra,
Erich Leinsdorf conducting, with
author Berkowitz to his immediate left.

METROPOLITAN OPERA

Wednesday Evening, December 4, 1985, 8:00

NEW PRODUCTION

The 191st Metropolitan Opera performance of

WOLFGANG AMADEUS MOZART

Le Nozze di Figaro

Opera in Four Acts

Libretto by Lorenzo da Ponte

Conductor:	James Levine
Production:	Jean-Pierre Ponnelle
Set and Costume Designer:	Jean-Pierre Ponnelle
Lighting Designer:	Gil Wechsler

Characters in order of vocal appearance:

Figaro	Ruggero Raimondi
Susanna	Kathleen Battle
Don Bartolo	Artur Korn
Marcellina	Jocelyne Taillon
Cherubino	Frederica von Stade
Count Almaviva	Thomas Allen
Don Basilio	Michel Sénéchal
Countess Almaviva	Carol Vaness
Antonio	James Courtney
Don Curzio	Anthony Laciura
Barbarina	Dawn Upshaw

Chorus Master:	David Stivender
Musical Preparation:	Janine Reiss, Dan Saunders, and Max Epstein
Assistant Stage Directors:	Phebe Berkowitz, Paul Imbach, and Lesley Koenig
Prompter:	William Vendice
Recitative Accompanist:	Dan Saunders

This production of Le Nozze di Figaro was made possible by generous and deeply appreciated gifts from the Gramma Fisher Foundation, Marshalltown, Iowa, and The Eleanor Naylor Dana Charitable Trust.

The Metropolitan Opera is pleased to honor violist David Berkowitz this evening on the occasion of his fiftieth anniversary as a member of the Metropolitan Opera Orchestra.

Light levels have been adjusted for this evening's performance in preparation for the videotaping of the Saturday afternoon, December 14 performance. The program will be simulcast on April 23, 1986, in the "Live from the Met" series, on WNET/13 and the entire Public Broadcasting Service. We regret any disturbance.

Baldwin is the official piano of the Metropolitan Opera.
Latecomers will not be admitted during the performance.

Program for a Met performance of "Le Nozze di Figaro" on Dec. 14, 1986, signed by James Levine and members of the orchestra, in honor of violist David Berkowitz's 50th anniversary with the Metropolitan Opera Orchestra.

MET ORCHESTRA LOCKED OUT

The Metropolitan Opera Association has LOCKED OUT its orchestra. This is another example of Met management's irresponsible brinkmanship. More than 15 fruitless negotiation sessions have been held since January, 1980. The orchestra asked for negotiations to start as far back as November, 1978, but no meaningful response has come from the Met management.

The orchestra generally has played a 6-day week of rehearsals and performances. On many days, work started at 11 a.m. and ended at midnight. The orchestra has proposed to ameliorate this heavy work load by reducing the number of performances per musician per week from 5 to 4. Even with a 4 performance week, the players would still work 5 or 6 days, with some work day spans of 12 or 13 hours.

Also still at issue are wages, health and dental benefits, per diem on tour, pension, and several other items.

At one time the Met Orchestra was the pacesetter for American orchestras in the classical field. The other major orchestras have long since leap-frogged over us with wages, working conditions and fringe benefits worthy of their professional and artistic achievements.

The Met management tried to make the orchestra the "whipping boy" in this case by announcing publicly that if labor agreements were not concluded prior to September 3, this season would be cancelled. By strange coincidence, September 3 was the day the orchestra was scheduled to start rehearsals.

We do not intend to be the "poor relatives" of the music world any longer.

The Met management finds all sorts of money for all sorts of purposes: stars, sets, lighting, costumes, etc.—but "poor-mouths" when its orchestra simply wants to narrow the gap between—not even catch up with—the other major orchestras of the calibre of the Met Opera Orchestra.

None of the issues between us and the Met management are new. They have been kicked around—and under the rug—by management for many years. They have stalled and dragged their feet without addressing *any* of the issues, even up to Zero Hour.

We regret any inconvenience to the public caused by management's short-sighted and self-defeating ploy.

MAX L. ARONS
PRESIDENT, LOCAL 802
American Federation of Musicians

THE MET OPERA ORCHESTRA COMMITTEE
SANDOR BALINT
Chairman

Met Orchestra Lock Out —
flyer handed out by musicians
during the 1980 strike

Sir Rudolph Bing
General Manager of the Met

Met Opera Orchestra members picketing.

Stalemate at the Opera

We were still in the old house when, in 1962, in President Kennedy's term, the orchestra was forced to undertake its most serious strike in my experience at the Met. The issues were always the same — better working conditions, more money, medical insurance, and pension. The entire house joined in. There was no opera and no way, it seemed, of resolving the issues. Even Sir Rudolf Bing was greatly concerned that this would be the end of his regime.

It was at the beginning of the arts program in America and, to a degree, of a government-subsidized Metropolitan Opera. President and Mrs. Kennedy were very much interested in the arts and much concerned about the stalemate at the opera. They intervened personally at the request of prominent singers, such as Robert Merrill, Rise Stevens, and Richard Tucker, who were worried about the opera and their own careers.

The President appointed Arthur Goldberg, the Secretary of Labor, to try to mediate this strike. We agreed to work with him.

On opening night he came down to address the orchestra. He was in full evening dress and top hat, and had come from Sir Rudolf Bing's box. Mr. Goldberg was very gracious and spoke to us in his Chicago accent. The orchestra was very happy and optimistic as we thought this would be the beginning of success in our negotiations.

His first words were, "Gentlemen, I feel for you. My brother-in-law is a member of the Chicago Symphony and I've watched the struggle he has faced, very similar to your own. I know what my sister had to endure during this period. Believe me, I promise you that I will do a great deal to help your situation."

Well, we started the season without a contract as we were encouraged about the future. Shortly after this, we learned that Mr. Goldberg was away on a good-will tour to Scandinavia. Whether it was a vacation or a good-will tour, we do not know to this day, but we were promised on hearing our fears that these negotiations would be prolonged and that his subordinates would work on a settlement.

When he returned from his Scandinavian tour he announced his findings, and the net sum of it all was that severance pay was eliminated and some kind of pension fund was established. Weak as it was, it was better than nothing. The rest of the benefit increases did not amount to much, no more than three or four percent. The musicians felt that our Mr. Goldberg was just another renegade, promise-making politician. He certainly did not do much for us.

We still had poor medical benefits in 1962. Just simple Blue Cross. However, more and more benefits were beginning to be read into the contracts, and our medical benefits were gradually improved to match other workers in the City of New York. This continued until today and I would say the benefits to members of the orchestra at the Metropolitan Opera are on a par with the best. The progress, nevertheless, was painfully slow.

In 1962 the contract was far from ideal and at that point we were looking for more time off for the members during the work week, a longer paid vacation, so that we could practice, study, and spend some time with our families. I do not think the public is aware that you must practice your instrument to keep up your skills in addition to playing on your job. There is an old story among musicians that says "your stand partner will know first and the conductor will know last," but you have to be very conscientious. This is not only to keep your job but for your own satisfaction and pride as an artist. Being a member of the orchestra was a constant challenge — new music, new productions, new conductors, and you really had to keep up. People do not realize that even though you play many hours in the opera house, you also play untold hours at home to hone your skills.

Many people, including other musicians, think the opera repertoire is comparatively simple compared to that of the symphonic repertoire. Nothing could be further from the truth. The Metropolitan Opera uses a limited number of operas from the existing repertoire of perhaps two hundred, and these are repeated many times. However, many of them are very, very difficult and they have to be practiced constantly. "Hansel and Gretel" by Humperdinck, which seems simple to the public, for it was written for children, has passages in it as difficult as some of the Wagner operas. Each year we have played it, I found it necessary to review it a few weeks in advance to play it properly.

Most members of the orchestra rarely had a day off until the 50's or 60's — certainly no time off during the day. You arrived at the opera house for a 10:30 or 11 AM rehearsal, and often did not get home until one or two in the morning, and then the process would start all over again the next day. This routine went on for years, but the contracts were becoming a little better. We now had a six-day week — the Sunday concerts were eliminated, which meant seven performances weekly.

The sole aim in the 60's was to get more time for our private lives, and to match the benefits of the symphony orchestras. By this time the symphony player had a maximum of perhaps four or five or five and a half hours of play in any day, three days a week. On the day of a concert only one rehearsal was permitted. The day prior to a concert, two rehearsals — in other words, three or four rehearsals for each weekly program. The Philharmonic has four services and four concerts unless there is some special event. Our services were unlimited. Management could call as many rehearsals a week as they wished. Double rehearsals were not unusual — one in the morning and again in the afternoon and then for the evening performance, all with different operas and casts.

Each opera performance can last anywhere from three to five hours, and an opera like "Parsifal" is six hours long! The entire day was occupied by travel, rehearsing, and playing. We had no time to rest our shoulders, lips (if one was a wind player), and above all, no time for personal freedom, something everyone needs. This was the big battle through the years. We wanted benefits all workers in every field had — coffee breaks, shorter work week, and certainly better pay. We wanted longer intermissions between acts to rest, and shorter daily hours.

Management always opposed us on these issues. We got no cooperation from them. We had established the precedent for all the American orchestras on how to operate to get better contracts as far as remuneration was concerned. We were considered number one in the field for take-home pay. As a result, the other orchestras began to demand better pay from their Board of Directors. I remember a conversation I had with Zubin Mehta who told me about the battles he had with the Los Angeles Symphony Board of Directors to convince them it was necessary to improve the monetary situation of the musicians.

The Board of Directors of the opera understood very little about working conditions and cared less. They were bankers, lawyers, who represented the largest corporations in New York — they were the so-called Four Hundred, the financial elite who made the opera "tick" as far as the contributions were concerned, but they did not like to pay workers.

There was a complete change because of the economy and the high taxes. It was left up to the general public to support the opera to a great extent. Management developed all sorts of gimmicks. They pleaded for funds via their weekly national broadcasts and the public responded generously, so we realized one way or another the opera would survive. However, the opera's survival did not solve the musicians' problems. How were we to overcome this battle to lighten this brutal schedule?

When the next contract change approached in 1964 or 1965, we could not come to any agreement, but we decided to work without a contract. The orchestra was very divided on this issue. Some did not want to go back to work without a contract, and some were willing to work under any conditions. They had families to feed and no-one had any reserve funds. It was quite understandable. The orchestra had heard of a clever labor lawyer, Herman Gray, who was a professor of law at New York University. Some members of the orchestra had occasion to use him for personal matters and recommended him to us. We engaged him ourselves. This had nothing to do with the musicians' union. The union would do whatever we wished them to do and would try to battle it out, but they rarely succeeded as they were not very effective at that time.

We continued to perform without a contract and in spite of many meetings, we were going nowhere. Two or three times, we rented a meeting-room near the old union headquarters on 52nd Street, but we did not know what to do to end the stalemate and the men were getting restless. The management threatened to close the house permanently — no opera at all, ever.

I made a speech to the rank and file at this hall. I brought to the attention of the groups that the excavation had been made, and the cement poured for the new Metropolitan Opera House between New York State Theatre, which had already opened in 1962, and Philharmonic Hall, now called Avery Fisher Hall. We were sandwiched between the two. Very imposing today, but then the area was one large square cavity. My suggestion to the membership was to take a walk uptown and look around. Many of them had never seen the excavation. It did not take much logic or extraordinary reasoning to see they were not going to leave this hole empty. The opera house was going to be completed no matter what.

Negotiations were going on at the same time about the disposition of the old Metropolitan Opera House. Management wanted to tear it down. They had worked out an arrangement to use the income from their ninety-nine year lease, and apply it toward financing the new house. A lot of money was available and anyone who saw the pictures of what the new opera house was going to look like must have understood it was going to be built even if Uncle Sam had to help. After all, it was an educational non-profit organization, and they had the benefit of no taxes.

Nothing happened in those two years of no contract. We could not come to any agreement. The building was finished and opening night was upon us. The morale in the orchestra was beginning to sink, and there were pressures from members of the families; younger members were more optimistic, but the older members had great financial responsibilities. We had to do what the public was doing about preserving their jobs and improving working conditions. I suggested again that the orchestra men and women take their families on a sort of outing and walk around this construction and take a good look at it. I was sure this would restore their faith that better things were to come. I believe it helped convince a great many members that the opera was not going to disappear, the opera would continue, in spite of management's threats to the contrary.

We wanted the same improvements all the time — more job security, and improvement in working conditions, and certainly more free time. The string players were more concerned because we played all the performances, every week. The leaders of the sections, i.e. concertmasters, were already getting one night off a week. Some were permitted to bring in a substitute player or arrange for a substitution with the associate first. This was an arrangement set with management some years before. But the rank and file of the orchestra had no nights off, or very rarely.

Most of the terms were agreed upon. The big unresolved issue was the nights off. We had a seven-performance per week contract, but there were woodwinds and brass who only had to work four nights out of seven. They had two alternates in almost every category — clarinets, oboes, horns, trombones, and so on. Their agreement was obtained because they convinced management the winds needed the respite from blowing their horns. They probably would have liked even less, but they could not very well complain in view of our position. The strings wanted a five-night contract and they would not give it to us.

The union offered us their lawyers, and offered to pay the expense. It had never done this previously, but we were distrustful of the idea because we did not know how much good they would be to us and we were not sure of the union. They always said yes to us and everybody else, but they were ineffectual.

We had hired our own lawyer, Mr. Gray, and he was a great help to us. He was the one who suggested to us that we play without a contract until opening night at the new house, and come dressed and ready to play, but also ready to walk out if our demands were not addressed to our satisfaction.

Opening night at the new house arrived on this vital evening. There was no resolution and we told them we would not play unless these issues were resolved. They rushed down to the big rehearsal room in the basement floor — Rudolf Bing, John Gutman, Bob Herman, and Herman Krawitz, and perhaps one or two other officials. We told them we had to have this concession. We were promised one additional night off the first year, which meant six performances weekly, and the second year of the contract half a night additional off — so we would have five and a half performances.

We settled this by taking a full night off every other week. Finally in the third year, we were guaranteed five performances a week. On occasion we had a Sunday performance, but we were reimbursed under our contract at double pay, and not too many objected to that. Some had the option of not playing the Sunday concerts at all. There were only five or six of these a year — benefit concerts or with artists who gave recitals with the orchestra.

This concession came about only because of the new opera house. There would have been no opening night if we'd decided not to play, and management could not afford that with all the dignitaries expected at the performance. These were drastic but necessary measures.

I can say unequivocally that this victory opened the eyes of all the orchestras, especially the "Big Five" — Philadelphia, Boston, Chicago, New York and Cleveland. They followed our lead and every negotiation they had was successful by using collective action.

With the advent of the new house a complete change took place in our profession. The industrial revolution a hundred and fifty years earlier had spread throughout the world with the invention of machinery. Conditions began to change for the workers at the early part of the century. The coal and steel strikes forced improvements in workers' conditions. However, this did not affect musicians. We were not involved in this development. We were still playing the same two hundred-year-old stringed instruments and four hundred-year-old bassoons.

After World War II we were aware of the changes in the working world and knew we had to involve ourselves in this process or we could not survive. Inflation rose to dramatic heights, and we were suffering more than anyone else. Musicians were considered artists, not laborers, and therefore had a difficult time convincing anyone they were entitled to a decent standard of living. This was partly our own fault. Artists think only of perfecting their skills and understanding the music. Remuneration is secondary.

BEHIND THE GOLD CURTAIN 89

Whenever the wealthy wished to raise money for a favorite charity, the first people they contacted were the performers and musicians. "Would you please contribute your services?" Everyone else got paid — stage hands, electricians, landlords, ticket-takers, ushers. Musicians, by contrast, were patted on the back for their wonderful generosity and genius, and expected to go home to spin through the refrigerator to see what there was for dinner.

Now that we had this complete breakthrough in 1966, our progress in negotiations spread throughout the orchestra world. The "Big Five" as I mentioned earlier fought to hammer out better contracts with their managements, including pension and other benefits.

We still did not work fifty-two weeks a year, but we were slowly and surely approaching that. Some other orchestras had beaten us to it. Many of the things they felt were necessary such as guaranteed annual fifty-two week contracts were not written in ours — but it was coming.

The 1969-70 season actually began in August with negotiations for a new contract. We were the big stumbling block: Everyone in the house was waiting for our settlement, as all the other contracts would then fall in line. That had been the procedure in the past, and there was great resentment on the part of the chorus and the other members of the company since the start of the season was being delayed by the slow progress of our negotiations.

In the end, we instituted our strike — the most disastrous and prolonged of all. It began in August and ended a week or two before Christmas. We had again engaged Mr. Gray, but he could get nowhere. The management made its "final offer," and threatened to close the house and turn it into an arena that could be used for events like the rodeo or the circus. Of course, management also realized that there would be nothing to manage if this happened, and the managers, too, would end up in the unemployment lines.

The temperament, temper, and attitude of the "top brass" became vicious at times. They made constant remarks to the press to denigrate the musicians, such as, "If the musicians do not capitulate they will be taxi drivers." One went so far as to describe us as only capable of being dispensers of ice-cream from a street cart. This particular remark came from Sir Rudolf Bing. This, about people who spent a lifetime perfecting their art. Sir Rudolf, until the very end of his regime, had nothing but contempt for the people who made the opera work, especially the musicians, because we seemed to give him the greatest amount of trouble.

Unfortunately, there was a split in the orchestra. One group took the advice of our lawyers to wait out the management; the others, who were finding it very difficult to survive financially, wished to settle.

We arranged an all-orchestra meeting at a nearby church, but the orchestra negotiating committee did not even attend. Accusations were made that they were not representing the orchestra, but themselves. It became bitter, creating a very dangerous situation that was much to management's advantage. There was a strong possibility that the season would be canceled entirely. Even Cornel McNeil, the President of AGMA (American Guild of Musical Artists) at the time, became involved on behalf of the chorus, ballet and other members of the company.

The union was notified of the serious split in the ranks. A meeting was finally called at union headquarters of Local 802, in the board room, with all the members of the executive board present to try to unify the orchestra.

Not all unions were as weak as we were. The stage hands union was very powerful. They simply laid it on the line with management. "We get this — or else." They were part of the Teamsters Union. Also their pension was handled directly through their union. Our pension was to come from the Metropolitan Opera fund. In the early years it was done on a contributory basis. We paid three percent of our salaries, and they matched us. Gradually, the percentage changed and it became a non-contributory plan.

This was a very difficult time for everyone. One of the warmest gestures was from Richard Tucker who addressed the entire company. We all suffered, but especially the chorus and ballet who had no strike fund or any income at all. Richard told us he had spoken to his bank president and made arrangements for anyone in need of money to go there and present proper identification as an employee of the Met and they could borrow up to $10,000 each to carry them through this stressful period. He personally guaranteed the loans! We all thought it was the most magnanimous gesture offered to us by anyone. He was an extraordinary person as well as a great artist.

A change of heart took place in the month of December, just prior to the holidays. To make it more palatable to the rank and file, management paid us a package of two weeks' rehearsal pay plus an extra week in a lump sum. This gave us a much needed sum of money with which to pay our accumulated bills.

In this strike period some men actually *did* turn to driving cabs in order to survive. Others borrowed money from the banks and relatives. Some musicians were able to earn some money teaching and playing odd jobs. In my own case, I was very fortunate to play with the Brooklyn Opera Company and various small symphony orchestras such as the Westchester Symphony. This helped to make ends meet.

BEHIND THE GOLD CURTAIN

Just prior to the settlement of the contract, we discussed organizing a benefit concert for the entire house. We had many very sympathetic people in the house who were willing to help us, including such artists as Richard Tucker, Renata Tebaldi, and many other singers, as well as conductors Leopold Stokowski and Leonard Bernstein. The concert was held at Hunter College.

Leopold Stokowski was most happy to do this as he had a "beef" with management. When we left the old house in 1966, he went on a campaign with a few others to preserve the old opera house. Once during a performance at the opera house, the great maestro turned to the audience, and in full view of a full house, appealed to them, beseeched them, not to allow the management to tear down the old opera house. He did not ingratiate himself to the management. They wanted and needed the money. Licia Albanese was another opponent of destruction of the opera house. She had many happy and successful performances there. In any case, the benefit concert took place, and it was a huge success.

The strike was finally settled and we had made a decent amount of gain. Many members of the orchestra felt the strike was a waste as we were not paid for five months, a loss of at least $7,000 each. The benefits gained were approximately three percent. Usually on issues of this kind, an added percentage was demanded and the settlement is usually one half. The one thing we gained was greatly improved medical benefits, and additional vacation pay.

By this time, the management was beginning to have more respect for the musicians as well as the other unions. They were all catching on quickly. We were always the leaders, the others were content to let us do the dirty work for them. The AGMA union, which represented the chorus, the singers, and ballet rode in on our coattails. They took the cue from us. They asked for double of our gains and ended up with the same thing we did. The stage hands could handle themselves.

Sir Rudolf was still our impresario and Anthony Bliss became the President of the Opera Association. He was schooled in the legal profession and was a member of a prestigious and powerful law firm. But his claim to fame was his father, the elder Bliss, a patron of the arts, who during the 20's and 30's swayed the "400" to come to the aid of the opera whenever necessary.

Bliss and Bing began to feud. There were a number of times when Bing made denigrating remarks to the press about the musicians that served only to exacerbate an already hostile situation. He stated we were qualified for nothing whatever without the Met. He said with contempt we were "only pit musicians," as though opera was easy and undemanding. This, to the greatest opera orchestra in the world, many of whose members came from the finest symphony orchestras to join the Metropolitan Opera. Anthony Bliss absolutely forbade Bing to make any more derogatory remarks to the press. It was at this time that Bliss thought in terms of establishing a new management to head the organization.

At the end of the seventy-first season a decision was made to engage a new General Manager to replace Rudolf Bing. It was Goeran Gentele, the Swedish impresario. Unfortunately, his tragic death in 1976 in an automobile accident necessitated change again. Schyler Chapin was appointed to step in.

After this chaotic time there were a number of strikes up until the present. The first one was in 1976, and the longest running strike after that was in 1980. Again we were out for about two months and again accusations were thrown each way. We claimed that management locked us out, and the musicians began to picket in front of the opera house. The opera used their powerful patrons to influence the police department, and every ordinance on the books was used to prevent us from picketing in front of the opera house, or on the sidewalk in front of Lincoln Center, which was city property. Everyone had a right to use it. We simply removed ourselves to the little park across the street. We had complete freedom there and were able to picket. We used many of our musicians to play daily concerts outdoors — trios, duets — anything to attract the attention of the public. We had our wonderful first trumpet, Mel Broiles, who probably did more work single-handedly than any four or five members to help. He made beautiful posters and played trumpet calls to attract the attention of passersby. It was like the call to God by the Salvation Army, with beautiful production and great trumpet playing.

Things had changed greatly since the early days. The union helped us out and gave us loud-speaker trucks to make appeals to the public. The equipment was much more sophisticated, and the union was much more aggressive than previously in helping the musicians as it had grown more powerful. It was completely different than it was thirty or forty years previously.

I give the most credit to the attorneys we engaged. I think I. Philip Sipser and his staff were superb. But the management was never able to hire the kind of labor lawyers who might have hindered us in our demands. Generally, we had better lawyers and came out ahead.

It was always the same old story. We were simply trying to improve over our past gains. Management, on the contrary, claiming disastrous financial circumstances, tried to keep us down. As is common in labor negotiations we asked, "Show us your books!" They always refused.

This reluctance had a reason behind it. Prior to this strike there was an announcement that the Met wished to establish a Hundred Million Dollar Endowment Fund to insure the future of the opera. There were many contradictory reports about this. Some said the opera was close to their target, and some said they were far from the goal, and that people who made pledges did not come through. The management's aim was to reach this goal by the 1983 season, the centennial of the Met.

We arranged a short term contract, two years instead of three, sacrificing some benefits so we could have a new negotiation for the 1983 centennial. We knew we had a powerful weapon. If we did not get what we wanted, no-one would be able to sing "Happy Anniversary" on opening night 1983. I am happy to say the contract was settled, and the pension made a large advance. From the string players' viewpoint, we had obtained a four performance contract like the average symphony orchestra players. This was a great achievement. Had I started that way in the early years, it would have made a vital difference for us all, as we could have had a more normal family life.

One more contract needed to be negotiated during my tenure at the Met. Looking back over my fifty years, I was enthusiastic about the provisions in it. The average Johnny-come-lately does not look upon it as we did. They take many of the benefits for granted, and do not understand how difficult it has been to attain the status we have today artistically as well as financially. The year I retired an added inducement was made. Anyone retiring in 1986 would be allocated an extra ten percent in pension benefits. This encouraged eight to ten members to retire that year. I could have continued. It was tempting, as the very next year the pension change was so dramatically improved, that had I continued to play at the Met for another year, I would have increased my pension by thirty-five percent. However, fifty years was a good time to stop. My colleagues wanted me to continue, and this was very flattering, but I wanted to relax and spend more time with my wife and children. There is not much time in a full schedule at the opera — it requires dedication and full attention.

Orchestra Personalities

Most of my fifty years in the Metropolitan Orchestra were spent in the orchestra pit, where there was always some drama, large and small, going on: conductors and artists arguing about their own problems in the score, and interrupting the rehearsals to do so; electricians interrupting the conductors and artists to set the stage lighting, and musician after musician passing through.

The pit was very wide, so we were referred to as "The 39th Street side" and the "40th Street side." And since we were so far apart neither side knew what was happening on the other, especially if the conductor faced to his right to admonish or speak to someone. If I were on the left, I could not hear the conversation. Many incidents helped to make the day enjoyable as well as miserable, and gossip was a favorite pastime. (It still is.)

At my audition in 1936 there were many people applying for the first time as well as older members who were reauditioning for reseating purposes or trying to convince the management to re-engage them as there was no job security at all. It was chaos.

The first violist of the orchestra was Albino DiJanni. There were legends about him, his past marriages, his past behavior in the pit, and his past appetite. He was less than five feet in height and very rotund. I would guess his weight at two hundred pounds. He was completely bald and wore thick glasses. I did not know who he was at the audition — I did not pay much attention — and I did not know his son John who played after him. John was a new member of the orchestra. His only affiliation before this day was to do extra work when additional violists were needed for the Wagner operas.

The old man had been given his notice so he decided to re-audition. The reasons he was on notice were that he had too much of an appetite for food and drink, and when he came in at night he was not always as steady as he should have been to play well.

When the audition took place I overheard the conductors saying they recognized the playing and that the "elder DiJanni was still the best. We must in all fairness re-engage him as first violist." Then came the next choice. Who would be assistant and sit with him at the first stand? They said that the young DiJanni sounded very well, they were familiar with his playing as well, and decided to seat him to share the stand with his father.

Well it so happened they were mistaken. The one they thought was Albino DiJanni was John, and vice versa. So they reversed the decision and John became first violist, and the father, Albino, was seated next to him.

Naturally, the father was very resentful that his son had replaced him. In addition he was embarrassed. He did not know what to tell his many "wives" about losing to his son. Later on, in performance, I saw the old man sabotage his son. For instance, in the middle of a "Tristan" solo, he would nudge his bow arm or crowd him so it was difficult to perform. John confided to me that as a good son he could not complain to management as he knew his father would be fired. He would plead with his father "Please, at least let me finish the phrase."

Albino DiJanni reminded me of a movie I saw some years ago about a ferry-boat captain who traveled between Gibraltar and Morocco, and who had a wife at each end of his route. I think Albino DiJanni could have been the inspiration for that story.

I became the father's confidant, and although I moved around the section during the first few years, I usually sat at the second stand with the other senior member of the section, Gabriel Peyre. I suppose our proximity encouraged our friendship. Albino always called me "Sonny-boy."

He had problems I did not understand in those days. As I look back, of course, I understand completely. He was legally married to John's mother. He may have divorced her, and then married another woman, but my guess is he did not bother with the details of legality. He also had a girl-friend, but referred to both of them as "wives." He was expected to spend at least two or three nights a week with each one of them. If he missed a few nights on the calendar, the wives became enraged and came down to the stage door of the Met. They wanted their allowances for one thing and an explanation for another.

Having been through this entrapment a number of times, he was very cautious, and enlisted my services on one occasion. He said "Sonny-boy, go out the 40th Street side, and see if my wife is out there." He did not say which one. Now the 40th Street stage entrance was the one we used to come into the opera house. The 39th Street entrance was generally used by the artists and the conductors. The telephone switchboard and the mail slots were on that side. Artists were often more concerned about their complimentary mail than they were about their pay-checks in those days. I went out the 40th Street side, and the woman he described to me was waiting for him. It was a Sunday night after one of our concerts, and he made his exit on the 39th Street side. She waited for him a long time, but no Albino DiJanni came out.

John was the son he had with his first wife, and he had another son with his second wife. Then there were a few daughters, but with which wife I do not really know.

If we came to a small town he always managed to get the first taxicab, and checked into the hotel first. One hotel in Richmond, Virginia — a beautiful place called, I think, "The Jefferson" — had a wide handsome staircase. While a hundred or so members of the company were still waiting to check in, there was Albino DiJanni descending the staircase with a girl on each arm. He must have had a certain charm that most of us did not have. In view of his physical appearance and age, none of us could understand it. Over the years up to World War II he had many escapades, especially on tour. Then he was either retired or forced to leave.

His son John and I are still great friends. He later became Personnel Manager of the orchestra and retired to Santa Fe, where he is enjoying his life to the fullest.

I had introduced him to Santa Fe when he substituted for me one summer season in the 60's. He and his wife Helen, a former Met ballerina, and their two grown sons and their families live there now.

When I joined the Metropolitan Opera Association in 1936, I had no opera experience at all. I was afraid of my shadow, and was awed by my surroundings. It was an era when any job was difficult to obtain and this one was highly regarded. My misfortune was to be seated at the same stand as a man named Francesco Biaggini, who was also beginning his first season. He had been substituting at the Met, and had extensive opera experience in Italy.

Biaggini was older than I, and could see immediately that I did not know many of the operas, although I played my instrument very well. He must have been very insecure about the job, but I did not realize it at the time. He tried to disrupt my playing in any way he could. He crowded me at the music stand so that I could not see the music clearly. In those days the violas played from the bass violins and harp side of the orchestra pit — that is the right side if you faced the audience. First violins, cellos and then violas. Today, the last twenty or thirty years, most conductors prefer the violas on the other side. Therefore, I sat almost facing the stage. I had to turn my head to look at the conductor, who was on my right. If I did not place myself at a certain angle, I could not see the conductor and the music at the same time. If the stand was placed properly you could raise your eyes as though you were wearing bifocals and see both the music and conductor at the same time. (I might add, I soon learned it was better if you *did not* look at some of the conductors.)

Since he was older, I was respectful and did not fight Biaggini. I just came a little earlier and adjusted the stand to my own satisfaction. As soon as he got there he hogged the stand and it was the same problem again and again.

He had another nasty habit. He "goofed" many times — played wrong notes noticed by everyone in the section. He would look at the conductor, shrug his shoulders, and point his viola at someone else. He really intimidated me, as I was so young and inexperienced. This went on for three seasons. In our third season, we were rehearsing "Gotterdammerung." The second act of the opera starts with pages of syncopation for the strings. It is a slow tempo and is almost impossible to play in unison.

Everyone in the viola section was guilty, although I later learned you had to create this syncopated effect, not be too precise. I was probably "swimming" along with everyone else, and my stand partner. We were bowing differently, and he began to make a funny sound with his lips — tsk-tsk — as though he were chastising me for playing incorrectly. That was it. I had had enough. I stopped playing, took the music stand with my left hand and placed it dead center, where it should have been. I had a good view of the conductor, and played more aggressively as by now I was familiar with the parts and I made sure I drowned out my partner. He was completely lost, and I imitated the sound he had made before with his lips.

The men in the section became aware of my behavior and were laughing. They had encouraged me for a long time to handle this man in some manner, and not let him get away with his destructive behavior. This was not some childish spite game. If the conductors thought you were the culprit — playing badly — your job was in jeopardy. When the act ended I anticipated some reaction. Like every bully, however, he crumpled, looked at me timidly and said, "My dear David, what happened? Why did you do this to me?"

"Look, Mr. Biaggini, this has gone far enough. I tolerated your nasty tricks and aggressive nastiness and it must end if we are to sit together."

He kissed me — on my hands, on my face, much to my embarrassment. He said, "My dear David, why didn't you tell me? I meant no harm."

I answered, "You knew very well what you were doing, and now it is going to change."

This was the first aggressive move I made to establish my position. Later on others who sat with him had the same experiences and came to me for advice. He did things to cover his own inadequacies. Biaggini came in wrong and alone on a number of occasions while his friend Panizza was conducting, and he let him get by, but when it happened with Fausto Cleva, he was fired.

On my left I had Biaggini, on my right a cellist at the second stand, Serafin Cristani. Cristani was a likable chap, but he stationed himself in a certain position in the crowded orchestra pit, and would not budge an inch until he left the opera house for the day. My life was miserable, as I was squeezed in between these two men and I was too timid to do anything about it. I would beg him, "Please, just move a little bit."

Finally, as I gained more experience and was more secure in the job, I acquired some of their characteristics, and I was rougher and less accommodating than I ever thought I could be.

One night I was hitting Cristani with my bow as I played. I was placed in such a crowded position, I realized if the conductor saw me it would look as though I did not use my arms. I could barely bow and I could not hold the viola up properly because of these two stubborn men. Finally I told Cristani that he had to move. Well, one word led to another. He was at least six inches shorter than I, but well developed and stocky. "Look," he said, "if you don't stop hitting me with your bow, I will beat you up. I'm pretty strong and tough." Then he said something that made me laugh, but I was too naive to know if it were possible or not. He said, "Besides I have three testicles like Hercules, and I am as strong as Hercules."

I was in pretty good shape as I was very athletic in those days, and answered, "I'll see you outside the stage door after the performance, and we'll find out if you *are* as strong as Hercules." I waited for him after the opera, but he escaped out the other door on the 39th Street side. The next day he apologized and moved to accommodate me; we later became friends.

An orchestra is a group, a family of friends and enemies, and many eccentrics. Oboists in particular are a strange breed. Some people blame it on the pressure in the head while playing this difficult instrument. There seems to be a greater incidence of strange behavior among them.

There was one gentleman who had been a wonderful oboist, but who had run into ill health and was declining technically. He could not afford to retire as there were no medical benefits or pensions then. His behavior in the pit was very erratic. The oboe sound is heard above all others, and this man played everything except his oboe part. One day during a "Carmen" performance in 1938, Maestro Papi was conducting. Suddenly, I heard the oboe sound playing the viola solo, the cello solo, almost every instrument in the orchestra score, except the oboe part. I thought he was a genius, but Papi did not see it that way. He thought the man was either crazy or trying to mock him. Papi tried to stop him, but nothing worked, he played on. Needless to say it was an abrupt end of his career. Another case of "another musician biting the dust."

In the 1938-1939 season, we were performing "Faust" at a student matinee. The conductor was Wilfred Pelletier, who in those years was in charge of the French opera wing. One of his conducting characteristics was to bury his head in the score, his hands high above his head, and conduct. Seldom did he ever raise his head to look in the direction of the players. Either he was afraid he had missed something in the score he had not noticed the last time he looked, or since we knew he was not the most competent conductor on the staff, we think he was looking for the next measure. When he did look up he usually took a quick glance around the orchestra to see if the orchestra was still there — to see if anyone had walked out of the pit.

At this performance, we were at the end of the second act, when Faust is enticing Marguerite — he had not gotten to the actual seduction yet; he was trying to get into her little house — the music takes on a very calm, peaceful romantic air.

At the second stand in the viola section, the musicians were Gabriel Peyre, who as I mentioned before had already been there close to forty years. Peyre loved to tell of his past experiences and knew the stories of the operas. He also alerted the younger and newer men of difficult passages coming up, a habit he never got over. Thus whenever these difficult places came along we were so on edge they fell apart, and we soon discovered we best learn them on our own!

He shared the stand with a newcomer, Harold Elitzek. Everything was calm at that point in the musical score and the violas were holding long notes, and Elitzek asked Peyre, "What goes on, what's happening on the stage now?" He described the stage action to Elitzek, saying in a low whisper, "You know, at this point Faust is leading Marguerite into the bedroom of the house, and we know what happens — he is seducing Marguerite."

Peyre is telling him this and his sense of humor took over: he stopped playing, placed his hand on his right thigh and extended his index finger and his middle finger and inserted his thumb between, indicating how Faust walked out of the house after the seduction; he bent the two fingers and let his thumb drag, thus giving a very specific pictorial/anatomical illustration of what had happened.

Harold Elitzek collapsed with uncontrollable laughter. He laughed out loud, and his body was shaking. At that moment, Maestro Pelletier looked up and saw Elitzek laughing hysterically. Since most conductors are paranoid, his first thought was that Elitzek was laughing at his conducting. He was insecure, and some of the musicians had made it clear that he was not held in high esteem.

If the laughing musician had been an older experienced musician, he would not have dared to make an issue of this, as that musician could embarrass the conductor even more. However, Elitzek was a novice, it was only his second season, and he was very vulnerable to chastisement. Pelletier complained to the Board of Directors, and towards the end of the season when musicians were given their notice — the so-called "Five Week Notice Clause," which gave them five weeks to find other employment — poor Elitzek was given his notice; fired. I went to Leinsdorf and a few other conductors (as did other members of the orchestra) to defend him, but it was no use. No conductor would even admit to voting to fire him. Finally, I approached Leinsdorf, with whom I had a close friendship, and asked him "Who actually fired him?" He never told me, but he said, "Don't blame me because I like his playing. Next season I promise I will engage him to play all the Wagner performances as an extra."

Peyre never admitted or demonstrated to the conductors what had made Elitzek laugh. It would not have done much good and certainly Pelletier would not have believed a word of it. In the Depression economy this funny story was not funny — it cost a man his job.

Shortly after World War II in 1945, we acquired a new member, a Canadian cellist named Gabriel Kellert. He and his two brothers were very well-known as The Kellert Trio. The trio disbanded and Gabriel's brothers, the pianist and the violinist, went to the west coast of British Columbia, left the music business and became wealthy miners and businessmen. Gabriel remained a musician and B. F. Rolfe, one of the well-known radio conductors of that period, heard him play and invited him to New York to join the orchestra of his radio show: The Lucky Strike Hour. He soon became well-known around New York and applied to join the Metropolitan Opera orchestra. He was engaged and assigned to the very last stand of the section. He became closely attached to me because I was a sucker for a misfit. Anyone who could not get along with others came to me, and I always tried to help.

Kellert was about five feet one inch tall and very obese, had slant eyes, and a mischievous look. He was completely bald and very good-natured — everyone would admit that.

We soon discovered that he had a few vices. How many, none of us really knew at the time. He was a devoted card player, and knowing very little about cards myself then, whenever I observed these games at intermissions, I noticed strange maneuvers, but did not understand them.

Whenever they played poker and gin, he would put three cards in the middle and draw others in such a manner that no one knew if he had three or ten, or he would put in four and take out five! He was expert at manipulating the cards. When it came to the tricks of card-playing, he knew them all. He was a crook, but he was an artist at it.

If he took a guy over, he would buy the poor guy a dinner. One of his tricks was to invite someone to the most lavish restaurants in New York. Once he took one of the oboists to The Chambord, at that time one of the most expensive restaurants in New York. He had won at least $50 from this poor guy in a gin game, an enormous sum then, and took him to dinner. The check was $100 so the oboist was even. But Kellert confided to me, "I won $50 dollars from him, and spent a hundred, but P.S., I walked out and didn't pay the check." He did this often. He would invite many musicians and walk out without paying. He said, "Look, if I'm caught, I'll tell them I forgot." Little did he know the law.

However, often he would pay willingly. He always walked around with a $1,000 bill in his wallet, so no one could pick him up for being a pauper or a vagrant. Once in Dallas, he invited fifty men to dinner between the matinee and evening performance at The Golden Pheasant, one of the best restaurants in the city. The check was at least $700 to $1,000 and he was happy to pay it.

In Cleveland, one of the last stops on our tour that season, he asked eight men to join him for dinner, and asked them all to contribute their share. It was a barbecue place. He had collected the money already from everyone, and walked out without paying the check. A little later other members of the orchestra came into the restaurant and the owner said, "I think a group of people from the orchestra came in for a snack and forgot to pay the check." When the manager of the restaurant described the leader of the group, all immediately knew it was Kellert.

The next morning we were on the train to Atlanta, an overnight trip. This trip was in the early 50's. As we were approaching Cincinnati the first stop to rest and refuel the train, a member of the orchestra approached by the restaurant manager told me about it, and I confronted Kellert.

I said, "You know you walked out without paying the check. You have *no* excuse. After all, they all gave you the money beforehand."

He was all prepared. He took a letter out of his pocket, explaining to the restaurant that he had forgotten to pay and enclosing a check. It was all made out. The stamp was on the envelope. The chances are he was not planning to pay unless he was trapped, but he was prepared. This was not a last-minute thought. It must have happened a number of times. He made the comment, "They can't arrest me for forgetting." I convinced him to mail the letter when we stopped to refuel in Cincinnati and watched as he did it to be sure. My analysis is that it was not the money. He liked the challenge of getting away with it. He did all kinds of things to make his life a little more interesting.

One of the funniest stories about him pre-dated his Met engagement. He played under Erich Leinsdorf in Cleveland during the war and he bought a big bus. I am sure he bought it for "peanuts" as it was antiquated. He bought it to transport the Cleveland Symphony Orchestra to U.S.O. affairs when transport was difficult to obtain and he charged the Cleveland Orchestra management an arm and a leg. But every fourth trip he'd throw in a free trip to show he was a true patriot.

This bus came with him to New York, and when he was engaged by the Met he parked it at Twelfth Avenue and 42nd Street and used it as his hotel. He lived in it, had all his belongings in it, and spent a few years in it until he finally got a legitimate dwelling.

The last tale I can tell about him is not a happy one. Erich Leinsdorf had befriended him as Kellert played very well, so Leinsdorf consulted him about fingerings and bowing for the cello parts. At the rehearsal the following day our first cellist at the time, Engelbert Roentgen, stood up. (His father was the noted radiologist from Holland, and he had been brought to New York by Walter Damrosch after World War I.) He asked, "Who put these bowings and fingerings in the parts?" Leinsdorf said, "I did."

Roentgen answered, "Maestro, I don't believe you were the one who changed these markings. They have been adequate for years during my regime, and I resent the fact that anyone without the authority to do so would make changes without consulting me."

It was revealed that Kellert was the one who collaborated with Leinsdorf and had changed everything. Roentgen threatened to resign and the matter was settled. The markings were erased and the originals were restored. Of course, Kellert did not endear himself to the orchestra, and this was only one of many incidents.

He loved to nap during a performance. The conductor could not see him as he was way in the back, under the stage overhang. Our personnel manager, John Mundy, shared the stand with him as he was often called from the pit to take care of other business. Kellert would stick his bow into the bridge and catch up on his sleep that way. Occasionally he would snore. Obviously the men in the section did not think he was a helpful addition to the cello section. Towards the end of the season another cellist, Carlo Pitello, wrote a letter on behalf of the cello section with the suggestion that Kellert should not be re-engaged. Every member of the section signed the letter including Janos Starker, then the new first cellist.

I do not think Starker was aware of this man's behavior, but he was willing to sign anything to please the men in his section. When the notices for firing came Kellert was on the list to be terminated at the end of the season.

The reviewing committee met to see if the reason given for firing a man was valid. Other members of the section were invited to this meeting to see if they could substantiate or refute the reasons for termination. We listened to a number of other cases, and when we came to review Kellert's case I realized a lot of the complaints were just personal dislike and a lot of charges of incidents that had occurred in other sections of the orchestra too. None of us were angels. When the testimony was over I made one of my lengthy speeches to the effect that it was the duty of the nine committee members to save a man's job, not to help fire him. It was bad enough we had to deal with the conductors who many of us thought were our worst enemies. They often accused us of non-existent faults to preserve their own positions at the Met. I told the men we should consider this and not get the orchestra to help the Met fire a man. Let the petition die if possible, I said, pointing out that he was worthy enough to be hired on the basis of his playing in the first place. Besides he was a sick man with very high blood pressure. I felt sorry for him and, above all, I felt honestly that we had to do everything to protect a man's job.

After the meeting broke up about four in the morning, everyone in the cello section voted to let him go. The next morning Starker, with whom I had become close friends, apologized to me. He said, "I didn't realize everything you said about protecting a man's job was absolutely true. Take my name off the list." I appreciated his acknowledgment, and he complimented me for bringing this to his attention. Starker told me that he was so disturbed after my talk that he had had a very sleepless night.

This situation did not resolve until a later date. I discussed the matter with other members of the orchestra and realized there was no good solution. I spoke to Kellert and said, "Gabe, the cards are stacked against you. There's a good chance, as you well know, that your contract will not

BEHIND THE GOLD CURTAIN

be renewed next year. If you care to listen to me, my recommendation is to write a letter of resignation and step down without waiting to be fired. Certainly you don't need the money. I know it, and you know it, and I think this job alone can kill you in view of the poor state of your health."

He took my suggestion and wrote a letter of resignation the very next day, and at the end of the season retired from the Met and joined the Baltimore Symphony where he spent the last few years of his life. I heard stories from the members of the Baltimore Symphony about him. He did not change. He was still a card shark, and always found a way to pocket an extra "buck" illegally. He would pocket four dollars but he would pay back double the next day by buying an expensive gift or a fine dinner.

Isadore Blank joined the Metropolitan Orchestra as first trumpet in 1938, two years after I did. He was a very talented player. And although he did not have the technique of Mel Broiles, his sound in "Parsifal" on sustaining a long note was so beautiful it made your heart cry.

He was a plain little Jewish boy from the lower east side whose father had a music shop. He dealt with all the musicians downtown who were looking for bargains. Izzy once bought me a trumpet for my son Robert for $35.

Everything Izzy Blank said came out comically even though he was entirely serious. One Saturday evening, for example, we performed Beethoven's Leonore overture in a "Fidelio" performance. The overture starts with a very difficult French horn passage. Our first hornist, Joseph Avalone, was a mild-mannered man, never lost his temper, never got excited in the pit or anywhere else, and was said to have a faster "lip" than Bruno Jaeneke of the New York Philharmonic, who was Toscanini's favorite. He did, however, have a terrible stutter.

The second hornist was a fellow named Gustave Roberts, a race-horse nut, short, semi-bald, and always working on the racing form, even in the pit. The third horn was Luigi Caputo, and the fourth horn was Sylvio Coscia, an excellent musician who later left the Met to become a professor at the New England Conservatory of Music when Gunther Schuller was its head.

During this time, I am sorry to say, the horns in the orchestra would "crack" — that is, they'd produce this unpleasant sound, which occurs when the pitch does not hold. The horns cracked a number of times that evening.

The next day the review in the *New York Herald Tribune* was posted on the bulletin board criticizing the frequent "cracking" of the horn section. (The critic was Francis Perkins, who would often sleep through a concert or opera and write a review about it in detail for the next edition.)

At the first intermission of the Sunday concert, the article was brought to the attention of the first hornist. Now it was never clear which horn "cracked." It could have been one or all four. There were perhaps twenty-five men left in the orchestra room; most get lost at intermission to play cards or chess, or go to the washroom.

The first hornist read the article and was so angry he completely lost his stutter! His speech came out spontaneously and quickly and he said half in Italian and half in English that the critic was "stupido — doesn't he know this is one of the most difficult spots written for horn?"

This man, so gentle, so sweet, was so angry that he backed away about four feet from the brick wall, where the article was posted, and threw his horn at the wall. It was like throwing a Strad. The horn was shattered, but he did not care. Dead silence. Everyone stood immobilized in shock. This did not upset Izzy Blank. In his serious-comic way, he bent down, picked up the battered horn and said to Abalone, "Don't worry, Joe, my father will fix it for you cheap."

The next day the critic amended the article by saying he inadvertently forgot to mention that "this is one of the most difficult horn parts and the Metropolitan's horn section in spite of the previous evening's mishap was a fine one."

Daniel Falk was an aggressive man, and entirely self-oriented. He used anyone he could for some service or favor to himself. He had befriended many of the European conductors before he came to the United States from Vienna where he had met them during his stint at the Vienna Opera.

At the end of the opera season he would find out which famous conductor was booked on a steamship to Europe, Fritz Reiner or George Szell, for example, and managed to book passage on the same steamship. He always took the very cheapest cabin, on the lowest deck, Tourist Class, and carried a doctor's note saying he could not eat certain foods. This way he was granted permission to dine with his pals, the conductors, or whomever he knew traveling in First Class. Then he would tip the deck steward to reserve a deck chair for him on the upper deck. As he was an excellent chess player, he spent each day playing chess and conversing with the conductors.

When it was time to retire he descended through the bowels of the ship to his cabin. But, in the course of the chess game, he would steer the conversation to stocks and bonds, and other financial matters, about which he knew very little. The conductors would then refer him to their own brokers, and as many of these foreign conductors had brokers who put American investment advisors to shame, Falk built himself a fortune. He

BEHIND THE GOLD CURTAIN

told me himself how he had managed all this.

To my knowledge he never spent any of it, and he spends his time to this day (he is in his 90's) waiting for the arrival of the daily mail so that he can clip coupons and count his money. He has no family, never gave to any charity, and never made any friends. He was not a nice man, and not popular with his colleagues. Most of us were sure he was a management spy, and he was heartily disliked. But, as usual, I felt sorry for him, and he did talk to me.

He played in the second violin section for approximately thirty years. We knew his hearing was not good, and figured that this may have accounted for his social problems. We found later that he was completely deaf; when the conductors found out, he was fired.

Gregory Ginsberg and I were friends. He was an aggressive European too, but he was also very funny. When I met him he had been at the Metropolitan Opera for some thirty years. Prior to that he was a member of the Andre Kostelanetz orchestra. His English was atrocious! It was heavily accented with what seemed like Polish, and completely fractured. I would ask him, "Gregory, you are an intelligent man, and you have been in this country for many years. How is it you have never learned to speak proper English?" I discovered later on that his Polish was almost as bad as his English. Obviously, he had little basic education. But he was not stupid by any means and he knew he was funny, although he did not mean to be. We often shared snacks after the opera performances and were usually joined by two or three colleagues. One night in Atlanta, Georgia, we were at a restaurant, and the waitress came to take our orders. Gregory said in his very poor English, "Miss, I vuntyou should bring me two hemboorgers und vun ruh." She brought two rolls, two hamburgers; one grilled and one raw. It took about twenty minutes to make her understand he meant "two hamburgers on one roll" after a great deal of commotion and laughter on our part.

In 1957, I was invited by Antal Dorati to join the Minneapolis Symphony as a guest member on a world tour. A number of Metropolitan Opera members were invited for this special engagement and Gregory Ginsberg was one of them. Most of the regular Minneapolis Orchestra members were mid-westerners and had never encountered anyone like Gregory before. When we reached Belgrade, Yugoslavia, our last stop, we were in the dining room of the finest hotel in the city. Many foreign dignitaries were there, especially from the eastern bloc, along with the entire Minneapolis Orchestra. It was September and Gregory ordered steak tartare. Apparently he had never seen that on menus in the United States and when they brought it out, he was so enthused he picked up the platter and circulated around the dining room to eighteen tables shouting, "Look vot I got! Steak Tahtah!" It was as though he had the forbidden fruit only God gave to the chosen few in Eden.

He was compulsive about cleanliness. He always came into the orchestra pit early. I was usually there, too, as my train schedule brought me there at least a half hour before the evening performance. I was on the other side of the pit, but I could see him. He came in with a can of cleaning fluid, a rag, a whisk broom and one or two other cleaning accessories. By this time, we had changed from the rattan seats to cloth. With Renuzit cleaning fluid, he cleaned the chair and the seat. Then he would put his violin case, which usually had a canvas cover, on top of the chair, again cleaning the case with this fluid. Then he took the whisk broom and swept the floor and everything around him. Last, he rearranged the seating for the first violin section, already put in place correctly according to marks on the floor by the librarian. He would arrange the chairs so that no one could possibly come into physical contact with him. At the performances, the musicians around him found themselves in rather uncomfortable seating, but no one protested to management as they understood his compulsion.

Another violinist, Joseph Geiger, had a similar habit. He was very gentle and well-liked by all the orchestra members. He had a little nail brush and washed his hands at least a dozen times a day for at least ten minutes each time — over and over. I wondered why. He was a shy man, and I knew he was not doing this to impress anyone. I learned later that prior to his arrival in the United States he had been in a Nazi concentration camp, sleeping on a concrete floor, in dreadful conditions. He had also developed a nervous tic from his ordeal and his head shook constantly.

He and his stand partner, another Viennese, Ludwig Vickles, as a gag, would turn the parts upside down and still play perfectly. They knew everything from memory, much to our amazement. As a result, Geiger spent most of his time watching the stage and little time looking at the conductor. Fritz Reiner noted this and tried to have him dismissed. The violin section appealed to Reiner on his behalf to say he knew the parts thoroughly, but Reiner said, "He plays with such inattention, I would like a man who is more cooperative and orderly." But we did save his job and he remained until his retirement some years later.

The Met on Tour

The early tours were made on the old-fashioned Pullman trains. The trains supplied were usually antiquated rolling stock. There were two seats facing each other, an overhead berth or bunk was pulled down and made up by the Pullman porters prior to bedtime. The custom was to let the older men get the lower berths and let the young men climb the ladder to the upper berth.

Needless to say, more men suddenly became older or indisposed and claimed they could not possibly climb the ladder, or they worked out some deal to get the lower berth. The lower berth was far more comfortable and had the benefit of a window. You could pull up the shade and read, while the upper berth was like a dungeon.

Our traveling was very primitive then. We fought for roomettes in our strikes. They had been available for many years, but it was more expensive for management and, of course, they would not pay for it. We finally gained the change as one of our contract conditions later on.

Each man got a roomette, which was six to seven feet in length, and had a little cubby washbowl. It was comfortable — you could live in it. There were times when we had two or three days without stops or playing, when we traveled from Texas to California for instance. We used the roomette as our hotel as we went from town to town.

Everyone was assigned a particular space, which was kept throughout the tour. The train waited in the rail yard until the performance was over.

It was quite an experience getting into the dining car. We waited in a line that wound through three or four cars. Generally, the air conditioning, such as it was, failed and once we got into the dining car, it was not unusual to find they had run out of food. Often we could hear the chefs arguing about the heat in the cooking area.

There were at least 400 people in the company and two sets of trains. The chorus and ballet traveled in one train, and the orchestra, conductors and singers traveled in the other. We got to know each other on these trains, and friendships were made in our close quarters. The conditions were not ideal, however, as we had to wait on line for hours for meals on these long runs, and although with the addition of the roomettes it was better, it was still uncomfortable.

We stayed in large cities for longer periods. When I joined the opera in 1936, we stayed in Boston for two weeks, so we used hotels. The next stop was Cleveland. This was a week's stay. The third stop was Atlanta at magnolia time, the early spring. From there we went to a split week — half in Memphis, and the other half in Dallas. Three days in each city.

Before the 1960's, we spent a few days in Houston. We also went to New Orleans, but that has been cut out of the tours for at least thirty years. We would then go north to Minneapolis for a week, then a week in Detroit. Occasionally we would make an overnight stay in Rochester, New York, and then head directly home.

But on these overnight stays when we still used trains, we began to perform in college towns. Bloomington was one of our favorite spots, the home of Indiana University. At Bloomington they welcomed us with open arms and we were put up in the newly built dormitories. We got the first crack at them before the students began to use them. Unfortunately, I heard later that the facilities were not left in pristine condition by the Met members. We would occasionally incorporate Lafayette, Indiana, the home of Purdue University. An important advantage of the stays in the college dormitories was the use of the school cafeterias. This was very helpful in an unfamiliar town. We did not have to hunt for a place to eat.

When we performed only once in a city we used the train as our hotel. Since the trains were exclusively for the Metropolitan Opera, if we stayed in a city like Cleveland, we could leave our personal possessions onboard. We would take off only what we needed for the day. If the train arrived early in the morning, we could remain on it until lunch time. Then the train was moved to a separate siding to allow normal train traffic to go by. A notice was posted to tell us at what hour the trains would be available for boarding.

The hotel in Cleveland was directly opposite the mammoth auditorium center, a new convention hall used for boxing and seating between 10,000 and 12,000 people. The naked eye could not see the end of the auditorium, you needed opera glasses. The seating was on risers and there was a balcony all around the auditorium.

Not all members performed each night in each town, so they had to wander around the town like gypsies, unless they were willing to stay on the train on the siding. This was not very feasible as the trains had to be cleaned and serviced.

When we switched to roomettes it was a great improvement for us. It was very difficult for us to win this point during our contract negotiations as the opera management was still trying to save money. I never did find out if it was merely coincidence or not, but the younger men usually found themselves in the roomettes located directly over the wheels and when the trains bounced, you felt it the most if you were in that location. We all tried to obtain a roomette at the center of the car, or the very end of the car to avoid the over-the-wheel place on the car.

That was my first introduction to sleeping pills. I visited my physician and explained the problem. I would spend the entire night bouncing over the wheels and counting sheep. Other members used the compartments to play cards all night long. There was usually one parlor car on the train, also used to play cards all night. Some men used the men's lounge. The toilet facilities were there, but there was an entrance area, where it was possible to sit, and eight or ten men would usurp that space too for playing cards. Most musicians were either expert at cards or just loved to play. If you were unlucky enough to be rooming next to a group of card players, you were kept awake all night with their chatter.

For some members of the company the tours were opportunities for rendezvous. It was not my concern but I heard tales of escapades that took place between the sexes in the compartments.

Eating was also a problem. Not every hotel had a restaurant or a fine dining room, and many of the men found this was the most expensive way to eat. Do not forget we were grossly underpaid while on tour. Our per diem allowance for food and hotel was only $10 or $15 a day, and we had to save as much as we could to take care of extra expense such as laundry, telephone, and any additional incidental expenses. Today, the per diem is more like $100 a day, a more reasonable sum to take care of needs more comfortably.

When the opera performance was over we were hungry. We had not eaten since around 5PM, and the opera performance ended about midnight. There were no fast food places in those days like McDonald's or Burger King. The only fast food I remember from that period was the White Castle. Very few restaurants were open at that hour. Strangely enough in large cities like Cleveland and Atlanta all the restaurants closed early.

Most performances took place in the center of town, so when the performance was over, we all made a mad dash for a White Castle hamburger. I soon learned the older experienced members made a point of bringing food from home at the beginning of the tour. They brought enough to last at least a week.

We were only permitted one valise. It could be any size and it contained all your personal possessions for the entire six-to-eight week tour. Everything went into that valise. My own valise weighed something like a hundred pounds. My tuxedos and all my personal possessions were in it. We carried our own instruments. A good number of years later the management provided us with trunks and instrument cases, so that lessened the load we had to lug around. Later on they also provided us with tuxedo trunks. Now we travel in style. The trunks precede the orchestra wherever we go.

We usually left in April and the weather was changeable, sometimes balmy and sometimes quite cold. So we needed a great variety of clothing.

One man in the orchestra, Bozzacco, played the bass-trombone. He was generally used to playing bass trumpet parts in the Wagner operas — the horn calls. He was a very valuable member of the orchestra as there were not many people who knew this instrument. He was a very good cook and he befriended me. At one time he wanted me to go into business with him to can his recipe for spaghetti sauce.

When Bozzacco left home for the tour, he left with a valise filled with food. As we were only permitted the one valise, I often wondered where he kept his clothes. The first night of our tour in Boston, Bozzacco invited Izzy Blank, the leader of the trumpet section, and me to come up to his room after the opera for a small snack. I wondered what kind of snack he could prepare in a hotel room. He opened the window; it had a large window sill as most buildings of that era did have, and out came a round package of meat wrapped in tinfoil. A few paper bags appeared, and then another and still another. He had brought along an alcohol stove, and brought about ten pounds of rollatini that he had cooked at home in Newark, and another ten pounds of meatballs. All this sat on the window sill. He would eat this until it was gone, then he would buy other provisions in the next town, and cook something for the following week.

So it was that this invitation to a "snack" turned out to be a most delicious Italian feast. Later on I learned that Sundays posed a big problem in these cities about getting fed. Nothing was open on Sunday, especially downtown. My first Sunday in Cleveland was solved by my friend Bozzacco and a group of friends, a trumpet player named Recigno, the father of the conductor, and another trumpet player, Cavalho. They took over the luncheonette of the drug store in the hotel. The owner was promised that nothing would be disturbed and they used the luncheonette cooking facilities to prepare meals fit for a king. This drug store could only accommodate perhaps twenty-five people. Word got around and everyone wanted to get on the list, but not everyone was that fortunate. They only invited the people they really liked. We paid $2 or $3 each including the jugs of red Italian wine they provided. I am sure they made a profit on the deal in spite of the low price. Believe me, it was a feast — chicken, veal, pasta, other meats, all you could eat. This became a weekly routine whenever facilities were available.

The younger men were more adventurous and when Sunday came we would investigate the town and managed to find an eating place somewhere. Sometimes it was a few miles from our hotels, but the busses were available. However, the feasts with these Italians was a special gourmet and intimate experience, and I felt honored to be told about them and invited to join.

The situation at night was bad. We had to scramble for food. The brass players did not play as frequently as we string players, so they spent Saturdays shopping in the local food markets, did their cooking for the tour on Saturday in their rooms, boarded the train Sunday, and they would snack luxuriously Italian style all week. Some members of the company never went to a restaurant. They found some way to prepare food. The reasons were two fold — it was difficult to find food late at night, and it saved money. On the first few days of the stops on tour, my younger colleagues always had the same topic of conversation. "How is your room?" and "Have you found a good restaurant?"

The procedure for touring was as follows: at the end of the season the travel department of the Metropolitan Opera gave us a list of hotels available, listing the prices. Often a special rate for members of the company was provided by the hotels. You were at liberty to pick any place you wished.

Many stopped at the YMCA and a few men had arrangements at a rooming house when we were in Atlanta. It was very inexpensive — important to us as we were trying to save money whenever we could. People who lived and worked in the town were permanent guests at the rooming house. It was not just the Metropolitan Opera people. This was my first experience eating commune style, reaching six feet for a piece of bread and three feet for some beans. However, the food was good home-cooking and included in the fee.

Getting from the railroad station to a hotel was a nightmare. Everyone would run out to get a cab, and in those days there were very few, so some people ran the four or five blocks to the hotel thinking they could beat the rush. They were in a hurry to get first choice of rooms and avoid standing in line. Others waited until the rush was over and took their chances.

When a group of us arrived at a hotel on the travel list sometimes as many as fifty or sixty at a time, everyone was anxious to get settled quickly. As a rule we wanted to stay as close to the performance hall as possible. Often there were forty people ahead of you on the line, backed out into the street. Then there was the business of your fully-loaded suitcase. Lug it in? Leave it on the sidewalk waiting for a porter? You certainly could not leave your instrument.

In Cleveland we performed at the Public Auditorium, which was directly across the street from the Auditorium Hotel. Naturally, everyone wanted to stay there, and this created more chaos than usual. Then there were the foreign musicians, the ones who came over as refugees after World War II. New arrivals were much more aggressive than we were. They did not believe in waiting politely for their turn. They just went to the head of the line and checked in, which angered the rest of us. There were a few "characters" among them.

One, a likable chap, was Gregory Ginsberg, but he would never take "no" for an answer. If you were twentieth in line you would see Gregory number one at the desk, already complaining to the clerk that "I must" in broken Polish-accented English, "I must have my room changed." When he was asked why, he would say things like "I can't stand the color of the carpet, and the sink in my room has the spigots on the wrong side: where the hot water should be, it is just the opposite." He would find everything wrong and the guys in line who had not checked in yet would become exasperated and start yelling "C'mon Ginsberg, let us get to our rooms!" The foreign newcomers were having their rooms changed before we had even checked in at all!

Then there was Daniel Falk. He would go to a first-class hotel such as the Hotel Statler in Cleveland, and ask for the cheapest room. He would brag to everyone he met he was staying at a first-class hotel with the artists and conductors. He did not mention he was in a cubby hole with no window or a small room not much larger than a broom closet. He did not care. He used his proximity to the conductors to get to know them personally and use them if he could for personal favors later on.

Included in our early tours for a number of years was the city of New Orleans. Even then in the 1930's, there had been some reconstruction of the French Quarter. It was fascinating for us — the marvelous restaurants and the unique lay-out of the city. Since New Orleans is below sea level their aqueduct system and sewage system are like that of the Roman Empire when aqueducts were built above ground. In the cemeteries the graves are built on mounds above sea-level. There is a monument on every grave, and each grave is at least four feet above sea-level. The climate is terrible — damp and humid.

When we left to go on tour, we had to be equipped for all kinds of weather. We left New York in early spring when it was still blustery. As we traveled south to Atlanta our bodies were subjected to enormous climatic changes. There was no air-conditioning then, and the temperature often reached the nineties in Atlanta and New Orleans. At the other extreme in Dallas we could be pelted with hail.

When we traveled by train, we really got to see the United States, and at the opera's expense. The modern flying traveler misses this. In New Orleans there was much to see, do, and especially to eat. In a bar called the "Napoleonic Bar," the owner had a huge collection of opera records of all the famous singers, and he played them continuously. The people who loved opera would go to the opera for four hours and then go there and listen some more. The opera company people also congregated there.

Most of the cities were not equipped with opera houses. In New Orleans, like St. Louis, Cleveland, and Minneapolis, there was usually a large arena which was used for various purposes such as conventions, boxing matches, and other sporting events. The seating was flexible. There were four or five thousand stationary seats and then more seating was added on risers so that everyone could see the performances.

We presented the opera in New Orleans for a number of years with great success. One Friday evening a performance of "Rigoletto" was scheduled, but three star performers canceled. One was Lawrence Tibbett, who was in no condition to sing — he was intoxicated, having visited one bar too many. A basso, Norman Cordon, who boasted he could eat four dozen oysters before a performance to enhance his singing, must have eaten a fifth dozen, and he canceled. Then soprano Lily Pons also canceled because of laryngitis. At curtain time, before the opera began, the announcements were made about the cancellations. You could hear the complaints and groans. Even though there were fine singers as substitutes the people wanted their money back and stamped their feet in anger. It was very embarrassing for the company.

The following afternoon we had scheduled a matinee performance of "Hansel and Gretel." It was customary to allow children to attend a Saturday matinee. "Hansel and Gretel" was practically unknown then by the average opera-goer and since tickets were not sold on a series basis in

New Orleans, people bought single tickets to hear their favorite operas or singers. The cancellations of the previous evening had been reported in the newspapers and by word of mouth. Only two hundred and fifty people came to the performance in that huge arena. The performance was delayed for half an hour and the management reluctantly canceled it. There were more performers than audience in that large theater. That was the coup-de-grace of the stint in New Orleans. The contract was not renewed and we visited one or two cities in Texas instead, such as Houston and San Antonio.

Arrangements were made for us to tour in Canada. They were eager to have us and there was great excitement about our visit there. We planned to visit Toronto and Montreal.

Toronto is the capital of Ontario and is the most cosmopolitan and commercial city in Canada. Again, there was no opera house. Arrangements were made to use their hockey arenas. We usually visited Toronto first and performed in the famous Maple Leaf Hockey Arena, which accommodated close to twenty thousand people. Their method of presenting the opera was to cut the arena in half. It was sort of an oval shape and one half was used as a stage, and the audience sat around the other: like a hard boiled egg cut in half. There was great anticipation in Toronto about our initial visit and the house was sold out. The Chamber of Commerce arranged a lavish feast after the performance and the entire Metropolitan Opera Company and all the important people in town were invited. Platters and platters of food were served, enough for at least two thousand people. There was so much food that, although I did not have the courage to do it, many of the company members took away enough food to last the whole week of the engagement. They bagged whatever was convenient and not leaking.

We traveled to Toronto each year for approximately ten years. A theater was finally built that was more appropriate for opera and concert performances, the O'Keefe Theater in downtown Toronto, the funds for it contributed by the O'Keefe Breweries.

A big problem to be solved on tour was the transportation and set-up of the stage sets. Occasionally we used the same sets used at the Met, but most of the theaters could not accommodate them. Sets were specially built for tours and they were dragged all over the country by a haulage company — Clark Interstate. Today most of the theaters are adequately equipped to present opera productions and the specially built sets are replicas, perhaps shallower or smaller than the originals in New York.

As soon as we finished a performance in one town, the trucks were loaded all night long and they were on the road the next morning to make sure they arrived on time at the next stop. This involved as many trucks as there were operas. Some of the opera sets did not fit on one truck and if there was extra space for storage in an additional truck, personal trunks and miscellaneous items would be added. One opera was unpacked at a time.

The backstage or whatever they called backstage in these arenas was a mess. You often could not find your way around. You had to be directed to the so-called orchestra pit. People were cueing in singers from every direction, and it was chaotic.

We switched from trains to planes in 1966. This change came about because the railroad equipment was beginning to break down. Also the special trains we used were not always available to us. Many organizations used these trains — circuses, sales conventions, rodeos — so management decided, finally, to change to plane travel.

Eastern Airlines became our first carrier. Eastern's administrators felt the publicity about its association with the Metropolitan Opera so valuable they contributed to the production of the Ring Cycle begun in 1967, and promised to underwrite the entire production. They did underwrite the first two operas and Rudolf Bing hired Herbert Von Karajan to direct. He was here for two of the four operas.

The tours had changed dramatically from my earliest years at the opera. The terrible quarters, berths, no air-conditioning, inadequate dining facilities — all had improved considerably. Even though we still used trains we all had our own roomettes, trunks for clothing and instruments, and better accommodations.

We had only two very long tours on the trains. We went across the United States to California through the desert in Texas, Arizona, and New Mexico until we reached Los Angeles, but did not stop at any town unless there was something interesting to see, or to service the train.

Once we stopped briefly in El Paso, Texas, the southernmost point in Texas, opposite Juarez, Mexico. The conductor told us we had an hour, if we wanted to cross the border. Five or six did just that and did not get back in time and the train left without them. Gunther Schuller was one of them. I never found out how he finally joined us in L.A. on time.

One member of the orchestra, Theodore Rattner, a violinist and escapee from Nazi Germany, carried a small hard-shelled cover valise he had brought to the U.S. with him. He always kept one or two salamis, a cheese that would not spoil too quickly, some tea, and a small alcohol burner. On a number of occasions as I passed his little bunk on the train, he invited me to sit next to him and enjoy a cup of tea and a slice of salami.

When we changed to planes, management took more responsibility for organizing the tours. Travel representatives were hired by management to be sure we boarded the planes on time, as well as the proper bus to the various hotels. Some hotels made special arrangements for Metropolitan Opera members, and buses were available when we arrived in a city. Each had a sign on it, like Holiday Inn or Hilton. Your personal luggage was on the bus and you were delivered intact to your hotel.

The instruments and trunks were shipped on a separate cargo plane. Our private luggage was placed in the hold of the plane, and was always with us.

By now, we were in the fast food era: McDonald's, Denny's — all these were open almost all night, so the problem of food after a performance was eliminated to some extent. Even the hotels had more facilities. Many of the better hotels kept their dining rooms open just for us, so we could have something to eat after dining at five and starving after a performance that rarely ended before midnight.

But now a new problem arose. Most of the cities were expanding into the suburbs and the shopping malls and better restaurants went with the expansion. The downtown areas were deserted after business hours, and we had to cab as much as five or six miles to reach these areas.

Most of us stayed at hotels close to the opera house, as we had to perform daily. Some musicians and singers, also conductors, performed only twice a week, and they could live where they wished, often at a luxurious resort in the suburbs where they played tennis, golf, and swam. In Boston, Cleveland, and Atlanta the auditoriums were downtown. In Atlanta similarly the opera house was in an auditorium in Fair Park, the site of a world's fair built in the thirties by Billy Rose.

But the change to plane travel changed many aspects of touring. You could drive to Boston or Washington in your own car if you wished. I often traveled that way and took a number of colleagues along. We shared the expense of the gasoline and tolls. The wear and tear on the car, however, was all mine. One or two colleagues were rather obese, and I suspect the necessary frequent changes of shock absorbers and springs had a direct relationship to the avoir-du-poids of these rear seat passengers!

Managing to get time off while on tour was an ongoing problem, especially for those musicians who had young families. We were away at least five or six weeks, and many of us had never been separated from our families. There were always emergencies — a child taken ill, an older parent in difficulty, emergencies that necessitated going home. Many of us left New York to go on tour with a great deal of unfinished business of all kinds.

The brass players and woodwinds did not have a great problem as there were alternates for each player, and they could arrange to cover for one another. Sometimes they joined the tour in mid-week, and some even managed a week off depending on the instrumental requirements of the operas.

The strings had a more difficult problem because we had no official nights off, and we could not cover for one another. There was one advantage, however. Many of the orchestra pits in the tour theaters were not properly equipped. They were never meant for opera and often not large enough, so that we knew in advance how many strings could be accommodated for certain operas and all the strings did not always have to perform. We then arranged to take turns on getting these nights off.

Some conductors insisted everyone be in the pit, whether there was room to play or not. They liked to see a mass of men in front of them. Many others paid no attention as long as there were enough players to cover the melody and the accompaniments. That was all that mattered to them along with taking their bows and curtain calls from the audience.

Since many of the young conductors and singers were relatively unknown outside of New York, the tour was an opportunity to face the public and perhaps be engaged by other orchestras in one of these tour cities. This did happen in some instances.

For example, Erich Leinsdorf was engaged as permanent conductor of the Cleveland Symphony Orchestra. Thomas Schippers, because of his Metropolitan stint, was eventually engaged as conductor of the Cincinnati Symphony. Maurice Abravenel became the most important conductor on Broadway. He introduced "Knickerbocker Holiday," "One Touch of Venus," via his friendship with Kurt Weill. His exposure at the Met led to his engagement as conductor of the Utah Symphony. Max Rudolf made a fine career for himself during the Bing regime. He rose from being a backstage pianist in Germany to the Metropolitan Opera as accompanist and coach. When he left the Met he wound up in Cincinnati and later became musical advisor to the Dallas Symphony and became the head of the conducting department of the Curtis Institute of Music.

Some musicians had no need to return to New York during the tour, but the whole issue was of no concern to management. They were only interested in having us available all the time because we were being paid. They wanted their money's worth.

During the first week of the tour we went to Boston as our first stop, since it is only two hundred and twenty miles from New York. If it was necessary for one of us to return to New York, and if we had a car, and if we could arrange to be off, we could get home.

We cooperated among ourselves to solve the logistics. The string players would play two consecutive shows for a colleague so that he could manage two days off. We covered for one another, but of course the further we got from New York, the more difficult and expensive it became to get home, so we could not cover for each other even if we wanted to.

The Touring is Ended — A Long Summer Ahead

In the early years, the opera season was very short. It was only twelve weeks in 1936-37, then sixteen weeks from 1937 to 1945, eighteen weeks in the late 40's, and then no more than twenty-four weeks in the late 50's with a few rehearsal weeks added to that.

When the tour ended in mid-spring, we musicians had a serious economic problem. For some it was more difficult than for others, as there was often no other income, no money put away. If there was a family to support there just was not enough money left over to last from the end of the tour to the beginning of the next season in October or November. One colleague of mine confessed that he had managed to exist all summer on spaghetti meals daily, plus some cereal and milk for the children.

The problem became less serious with the advent of improved contracts and longer seasons — twenty-two weeks in 1949. But when I joined the orchestra in 1936, many musicians were supplementing their incomes with additional work. These odd jobs were scarce. So you can imagine how grateful I was to find work in the summer of 1937 in a society orchestra that used strings. The engagement started in mid-April and ran through September at a famous nightclub in New Jersey — Ben Marden's Riviera.

Then there was the World's Fair of 1939. Many colleagues with ties to the contractors who hired the musicians for the various shows at the Fair, the railroad show, for example, a comedy show with Gypsy Rose Lee, and Abbott and Costello, and the Aquatic Show, found employment in those orchestras. They also had a nightly trumpet fanfare, and they used many trumpet players for that.

Our piccolo player at the Met returned to his home town, Philadelphia, and found odd engagements there. The first stand men and solo winds and brass players were affiliated with schools and music conservatories and had many private students to help them get by.

As the season was extended, it became less difficult to survive this long hiatus. In the 60's, for example, we started a summer season at the Lewisohn Stadium at City College in upper Manhattan. When that ended because of the deteriorating neighborhood and the shrinking audience, the city park concerts were inaugurated with corporate sponsorship.

Then, in the mid-60's, vacation benefits were added to our contracts. Up to this point we had had no paid vacation. We started with two or three weeks; gradually, it was extended to a five-week period that began in early July and lasted until the first week of August — still not a full year of employment, but considerably better than before.

Later another improvement was added — a feature known as a S.U.B., or Supplemental Unemployment Benefits. Unemployment benefits were collected by us from the State of New York for the period of our unemployment, and the Metropolitan Opera management paid the difference between that and the base salary.

Back in the late 40's, however, we had none of this, and the monetary situation for most of us was disastrous. The season was not long enough for the salaries to last the year and our worst enemy, inflation, was rampant. The cost of living was skyrocketing — rent, food, everything. Those of us with families to support had to find a way to augment our incomes.

I was making a little with a few odd jobs, some teaching, and a few recording dates. After thinking of every possible way to handle my financial problems — I even thought of leaving music and going back to law school — I discussed my problems with my father. He suggested that since I had a good head for figures, I should study for an insurance license.

I had been approached by insurance agents and I believed in this protection for families, therefore I realized this would be a good avenue for added income while I continued at the Metropolitan Opera. I spent the summers of 1948 and 1949 taking insurance courses and received my New York State Life Insurance License in 1949.

I sat with this license for six months. Courses teach you about insurance, but they do not teach you how to sell it, and I was immobilized. I finally answered an ad at an agency and they helped me with selling techniques. One day a special four-week promotion was announced. The one who could sell the most insurance in that short period of time would win a Thanksgiving turkey. If you exceeded $5,000 worth of insurance, you could win other prizes too.

It was the turkey that inspired me. I sold policies to anyone I could grab — the butcher, the laundry-man and to myself on my three children. I won the turkey and more: since I sold $50,000 worth of insurance, I walked away with the top prize.

The word soon spread around the Met that I was a qualified expert on insurance. I still did not have the nerve to approach my colleagues and tell them what wonderful candidates I thought they would make for life insurance, but they soon came to me with their insurance problems. Later on, I found myself solving many of the insurance coverage needs of the members of the company.

As time went on, my reputation as a qualified insurance agent grew considerably and my income soon became supplemented by selling insurance to many of the musicians, singers, chorus, and ballet dancers. I did not solicit anyone deliberately, because I was slightly embarrassed about this phase of my life. My profession was music, a life-long dedication and the insurance was "moonlighting." However, there were many people who were sincerely interested in the welfare of their families, and the Metropolitan Opera provided minimal benefits, if any. These people wanted honest guidance regarding the insurance they already had and what they needed. I reported their problems to my associates at the Equitable Life Assurance Society, and they did the research for me.

In 1953 I sold the American Guild of Musician Artists, the union that represents ballet dancers, singers, and solo instrumentalists — 3,000 members nationwide — a plan for insurance coverage. They had had no insurance of any kind before.

An interesting sidelight to this story: Any foreign traveling group from what was then called the Iron Curtain countries, such as the Bolshoi Ballet touring the United States, was covered under this plan. At that time, it was forbidden for other insurance companies to insure these groups. We managed to do it, and while they were in the United States if a death or accident occurred, the Communist group was covered.

I was well on my way now, with insurance sales bolstering my confidence generally. We at the Metropolitan Opera still had no health plan and I pressed hard to inaugurate one. I brought colleagues from Equitable to speak to us, and they gave us the necessary information so that in future contract negotiations we knew what to ask for. Also, at that time, we had no instrument insurance. The orchestra discussed this and decided to finance a plan via a private agency on their own. We did this for two or three years. Eventually, however, this too was incorporated into our contracts. Even this additional income did not solve my financial needs as my total income still did not cover my expenses.

The real beginning of steady summer income came in 1953 when I had the opportunity to play the summer season with the Central City Opera, in Central City, Colorado. I loaded the car with the necessities for a family with three young children and drove to Central City for a stay of six or seven weeks. This also provided a summer vacation for my family.

It was a lovely spot — a small mining town forty miles northeast of Denver. There were abandoned gold mines where you could still pan gold, and many interesting stories about the area; the "Face on the Bar-room Floor" and the famous "The Ballad of Baby Doe" are about this town.

I soon learned how the opera company was managed. Fine young singers, some from the New York City Opera, and comprimario people or talented youngsters from the Metropolitan Opera, wanted to sing leading roles. They went to Central City Opera for those opportunities. The gentleman who ran the show was Bob Brown, a former member of the Denver Symphony and adept in managing the company. He came to New York each winter to engage the singers the little company could afford.

The musicians and singers who came from New York knew each other well enough to nod and say "Hello," but had never been able to spend any social time together. In Central City we were all living on a mountain-top 10,000 feet in the air with only two streets in the town, one leading to the center of town where everything was concentrated — the restaurants, the drug store, and the tourist traps. The other crossed town going in the other direction. Thus, we were in constant contact, either at rehearsals or performances or intermissions, and many of us became fast friends.

In the summer of 1953 the two most important singers at Central City were Lucine Amara, who was engaged to do a Verdi opera and Micaela in "Carmen." Amara was a young gifted singer who had moved from the New York City Opera to the Met and was engaged to sing the title role in "Carmen" along with the "Merry Wives of Windsor" for which a number of Metropolitan people were hired. The conductor was the assistant conductor and chorus master of the Met, Kurt Adler, and his associate Walter Taussig.

We spent two weeks rehearsing with this group. Most of the orchestra comprised musicians from the local Denver Symphony and from other orchestras in nearby communities. Our concertmaster at the Metropolitan, Felix Eyle, was responsible for recommending David Rattner, a horn player at the Met, and me for the job. Other Met singers were Brian Sullivan and Theodore Uppmann. We all brought our families and it was a lovely atmosphere for the children — better than summer camp.

Brian Sullivan was a young tenor just beginning a successful career at the Met and was boastful about the fees he received at Central City. They paid him about $5,000 a performance, more than what he earned in a whole season at the Met. (Some singers at the Met were engaged on a weekly basis or what is called a "plan" artist basis. They were paid a given sum every week for the duration of the season. Other artists were engaged on a per performance basis and were paid only for the appearances and the time necessary for rehearsal. It was not the way it is today when comprimario singers can depend on a substantial annual salary.)

Brian and I became close friends and he consulted with me about insurance. He told me he had been in an automobile accident recently and said, "Would you help me get coverage?" Brian was a lyric tenor whose voice later developed along dramatic lines. In Central City he sang Don Jose in "Carmen" and the title role in "Faust." He was rapidly developing into an important American singer. We only had a few, such as Charles Kullman and Frederick Jagel, but they were only used when some of the important Italian singers were not available.

Brian made his Met debut in the late 40's in "Peter Grimes" by Benjamin Britten. His success in that opera led to other leading roles, such as the duke in "Rigoletto." His voice deepened and he graduated to Wagnerian roles. He was told by the management that if he could become a good Lohengrin or Tannhauser, there would be a very important spot for him at the Met. He did sing half a dozen Lohengrins. Sadly, however, his career ended tragically in death a few years later.

Bob Brown tried to change casts at Central City every year, but there were some stand-bys who returned annually. Lucine Amara was one of these. She usually sang the lead in all the Central City productions. Ted Uppmann sang with us for two or three years, as did John McCurdy and Walter Cassilly.

In the late 50's we did an "Aida" and Beverly Sills came to sing in it. Cornel McNeil eventually sang "Rigoletto" in Central City. He and Frank Guarera shared the role. Jerome Hines had preceded me there. Then there was Morley Meredith, a very important bass-baritone at the Met today. Other visitors were: Charles Anthony, Thomas Hayward, the late Norman Triegle, Chester Ludgin, Roslyn Elias, Albert DaCosta, Sherill Milnes, and Justino Diaz.

I also had the privilege of working with Cyril Richard on "La Perichole," when we gave the premiere of "The Ballad of Baby Doe." The conductors who joined us in Colorado were as illustrious as the singers and included Emerson Buckley, Emil Cooper, Max Rudolf, Kurt Adler, and many others. I left during Emerson Buckley's regime having enjoyed the singular opportunity of meeting and befriending most of the younger singers who were later to make their mark in the opera world.

The Changing of the Guard

Edward Johnson retired from the Met in the 1949-1950 season and Rudolf Bing was brought in. The Metropolitan Opera Board of Directors had been seeking someone to replace Johnson and news came that Rudolf Bing had tremendous success at the Glyndbourne Festival in Scotland, both artistically and financially. He had brought about radical change for the better through his administration. Previously he was an agent for singers in Germany and Vienna and had graduated to this administrative position. He came to the Met in 1949.

I remember seeing him around the opera house in various capacities, observing this and learning that, trying to discover what he could improve upon. Finally, in 1950 he officially took over the leadership of the Met. He became our new impresario and remained there for the next twenty-two years.

Bing wanted to establish a true residential company composed mainly of American singers and international stars whom he could import from Europe when they were available.

The American singers became the foundation of our roster, and many of them developed into first-class stars. Unfortunately, they still had the competition of foreign singers, as the public was still trained to believe the great voices were buried somewhere in Europe. The opera public heard recordings of singers like Bjoerling, Tebaldi, Callas, Corelli, and on arrival, these performers had a tremendous following in this country. The tickets were expensive but the public preferred singers who came here for a short period of time then left for other engagements. The American singers were always available. They lived here, this was home, and they were taken for granted instead of being made the stars they should have been.

The period in the late 40's after World War II virtually eliminated

German opera from the repertoire. One, the singers were not available, and two, there was great prejudice against German singers because so many of them had been Nazi sympathizers and many had been Hitler's favorites. The management wanted no trouble, so Bing resigned himself to developing other phases of opera. He included more French operas and also introduced some novelties. His first opening night opera was Verdi's "Don Carlo" and he had engaged an entire cast of foreigners. This was the introduction to the United States of Siepi, a Brazilian soprano Delia Rigal, Fedora Barbieri the mezzo, and the conductor Fritz Stiedry.

The conducting staff was changing rapidly. Some conductors left voluntarily and some were not re-engaged. It was the hey-day of Fritz Reiner at the Met. Emil Cooper was considered a very important and valuable conductor and Bing brought in Fritz Stiedry. Bing knew him in Europe and since he himself was not a musician, he depended on Stiedry for guidance in selecting new conducting staff.

Stiedry brought back Fausto Cleva — he had gone to the Chicago Lyric Opera when he left the Met as chorusmaster and was in charge there. He had engaged Stiedry, and now Stiedry was returning the favor. Cleva inherited much of the Italian repertoire.

We now had three Fritzes at the opera — Fritz Reiner, Fritz Stiedry, and the most important and famous of all, Fritz Busch. He had been engaged by Bing's predecessor, Edward Johnson, and was known throughout the world as one of the most important conductors. He left Germany prior to the Hitler regime having recognized the coming disaster. Later his family joined him: Rudolf Serkin, his son-in-law, his brother Adolf Busch, the leader of the famous Busch String Quartet, and his son, Hans Busch, who became the head of the opera department of Indiana University.

Fritz Busch was expected at the Met in the seasons of 1951-1952. The Chicago Symphony had an opening for a conductor and Fritz Reiner was going to accept it. But I had heard rumors that we would not be seeing Busch any time soon. The rumors were true. One morning I arrived for rehearsal to find a telegram pinned to the orchestra bulletin board. It said, "MY DEAR COLLEAGUES STOP SORRY I WILL NOT BE WITH YOU THIS YEAR STOP I FEEL THERE IS ONE FRITZ TOO MANY."

Shortly after that Fritz Reiner announced his retirement from the Met and went to Chicago as conductor of the Chicago Symphony and we were left with only one Fritz — Stiedry.

All I knew about Stiedry before he joined our conducting staff was his connection with the New Friends of Music. This was a group organized by people who had escaped from Germany and Austria and wanted to maintain their artistry and resume their careers in this country. Artur Schnabel, the great pianist, was very much involved in their formation, so much so that among musicians the group was known as the "New Friends of Music and the Old Friends of Schnabel." They performed chamber music. Stiedry was hired as their conductor when a chamber orchestra was involved. These musicians did contribute to the musical life of this country as they helped popularize chamber music in the United States. They also helped popularize Stiedry, whose career was forging ahead rapidly in this country because of his association with them.

When he came to the Met at Bing's request, Stiedry inherited the role that Bodanzky had as top-dog in my early years at the Met. The orchestra was not impressed. Personally, I felt that whatever genius or gift he may have had was left in Germany. First of all he was getting along in years, and second, it was obvious he was having trouble with his ears. He always came into the pit with cotton stuffed into both ears. I could not understand why. I came to the conclusion that either he had some illness or infection, or the music was too loud. Perhaps he thought the cotton would absorb the sound and send a message to his brain.

He was peculiar in many ways, but down to earth in others. He did not establish a barrier between the musicians and himself as many other conductors did. He was friendly — too friendly, sometimes — and would waylay any of us he could and ask for an opinion of his conducting. Of course, what he wanted was to be told how great he was. I do not think he actually knew one musician from another. In addition to his deafness, his sight was not too good. He was very absent-minded and often disoriented.

Early in his stay at the Met he wanted to mount a new production of "Boris Godunov" by Mussorgsky but with a new orchestration of the score. There already was the original, the famous Rimsky-Korsakov version, and Dmitri Shostakovitch was working on yet another. He called upon an old friend of his, Karol Rathaus, a composer and head of the Music Department of Queens College in New York. Rathaus spent the entire summer on the score and the minute Professor Rathaus orchestrated a page, he would send it to Stiedry to give him an opportunity to study it.

We were rehearsing the opera in the preliminary part of the season. Stiedry would tell us he "didn't have time to study the new pages because they hadn't arrived on time." My brother, Sol Berkowitz, an associate professor at Queens College then, and close to Karol Rathaus, told me that this was not true. Dr. Rathaus spent the whole summer orchestrating the score and it was sent to Stiedry well in advance of the rehearsals. It was a very difficult score and Stiedry just did not learn it in time.

One of the funny things about Stiedry was his poor sense of direction. When he left the pit at intermission, he had to make a sharp left turn between the cellos and basses, then a right turn to go under the stage, and finally upstairs to his dressing room. The old Met was about eighty years old then, and underneath the stage it looked like the scene in the Lon Chaney version of "The Phantom of the Opera." Instead of making a right turn to go upstairs to his dressing room, Stiedry made a left turn and landed in the boiler-room where all the plumbing and steam pipes were located.

I had remained in the orchestra pit to fix a string on my viola and heard faint cries of "Get me out of here! Get me out of here!" A few of us went looking for this cry of distress. We recognized Stiedry's German accent and finally found him in the boiler room. He staggered out with cob-webs and soot all over him. We led him up the one flight of stairs and made sure he got into his dressing room to change.

Other conductors joined the roster in the 50's. One of the most prestigious of that era was Dmitri Mitropoulos. This was in the third or fourth year of Stiedry's tenure. Stiedry was jealous and suspicious of any new conductor who joined the staff, and always thought the new member was a possible replacement for him.

Mitropoulos came to the Metropolitan Opera after he left the New York Philharmonic post as permanent conductor. His introduction to us was the opera "Salome" by Richard Strauss and he was sensational. We had heard that he had a phenomenal memory. He conducted the very first rehearsal without a score. He knew every number, every reference, where to start and where to stop. He never found it necessary to consult the score. We were amazed. Few of us had ever had this experience with a conductor.

One day I met Stiedry in the wings of the stage. He cornered me and said, "Tell me about this Mitropoulos. How do the men like him and what kind of conductor is he?" I had nothing but praise for him. Most of the orchestra members felt the same way. Stiedry hesitated a moment and said to me, "You know this is a trick. He simply knows the melody and he wants to impress the orchestra." He went on at great length with everything he could say to belittle the man's ability.

I did not agree with him and I told him so. "No, Maestro. I'm sure it is not a trick. He has a phenomenal memory. As a matter of fact I heard he has memorized the New York City telephone book, and knows every name and place in it." When he heard me say that, the conversation ended abruptly as he would have had to challenge this, when he knew it was all true.

In every orchestra there is always a mixture of older men, middle-aged men, and new young members. The older members are better qualified to judge a conductor — how well he knows the opera, how little. The younger men are more involved in learning the notes and getting the opera into their ears. Also, they do not have the necessary experience to have a basis for comparison.

When Stiedry came to the Met he was playing new repertoire — it was to me, anyway. They opened the season with Verdi's "Don Carlo." I had never played this opera, so it was difficult for me to judge Stiedry's knowledge of it. Like many conductors he told us stories about his experiences conducting it — how he was the first to conduct it in Russia, the first to conduct in its original five acts and on and on. I presumed he knew the score, and I thought he was a capable replacement for the conductors who had gone.

Generally, for the first five years I respected his work, but later I changed my opinion. He did a version of "The Ring" cycle, and it was different from Bodanzky's approach. We had an all-new cast of singers, and I did not think it was an efficient rendition either artistically or vocally, but I may have been prejudiced.

Stiedry remained at the Met until the early 60's. He became ill on a number of occasions and there was one disastrous performance and broadcast of "Die Mestersinger." His eyesight failed him and he got lost. As we continued the second act of the opera it got worse. We were like dead fish in the water. Finally the concertmaster stood up and used his bow as a baton to direct and shouted "Letter C!" at which point we got together again. We just ignored Stiedry. He soon retired to Switzerland to write his memoirs.

I do not wish to conclude this story about Stiedry on a negative note. In all fairness to him, he came to the Met at the end of his career. He was well over sixty and his faculties were greatly diminished. He had seen his best days. However, conductors never give up unless they drop dead or are forced out of their positions.

In the case of Stiedry, our last experience with him was his leadership of "The Magic Flute." At the beginning of the second act of this opera there is a scene with full chorus and Saroastro, the priest, accompanied by a brass choir. They play a long call — the strings do not play there — but the trumpets and trombones hold these long sustained notes, then change to the next note. Roger Smith was our first trombonist at the time. He transposed his leading voice an octave higher than written. Perhaps he was a little tired or thought the conductor would not notice. Most of the musicians did not notice it as it was a simply orchestrated spot with a lot of unison playing.

About two weeks later Stiedry happened to see Roger Smith in a corridor backstage, stopped him and said, "Dear Roger, why was it that you did not play the leading voice in the chorale part for the trombones in the original register? Why did you transpose it an octave higher?"

Roger told him that he had been tired and thought it would be simpler and safer to play it as he did. (It is true that this is a notoriously difficult low note for trombone.)

Stiedry said only, "When we repeat the performance I prefer you play it the way it was originally written."

This proved that you never know what a conductor hears or does not hear, and also that Stiedry, in particular, still heard a great deal.

Dmitri Mitropoulos came to the Metropolitan Opera in 1957-58 and everyone who performed with him, perhaps with a few rare exceptions, was impressed. He was an extraordinary musician and a lovely person.

He made his debut in this country as a pianist, playing a Prokofieff concerto with the Boston Symphony Orchestra. The reviews were excellent and soon his reputation spread as a fine conductor, too. He was invited to guest conduct the New York Philharmonic. Soon after in 1937-38 he became the permanent conductor of the Minneapolis Symphony, replacing Eugene Ormandy who had become the permanent conductor of the Philadelphia Symphony Orchestra.

Mitropoulos guest conducted all over the world before he came to us. His reputation had preceded him long before he joined us, especially the stories about his phenomenal photographic memory. Even the great Arturo Toscanini thought him remarkable. Reports had circulated in the musical world that he was a fine conductor, who usually conducted with a baton, occasionally without. He became the permanent conductor of the New York Philharmonic Orchestra after the Bruno Walter days, and Leonard Bernstein was his Associate Conductor. (Soon after, Bernstein replaced him as permanent conductor of the New York Philharmonic.)

Many stories about Mitropoulos revolve not around his musical ability, but his generosity to fellow musicians. He spent most of his time with musicians even after he left his daily work with the orchestra, not at "society" events as most conductors did.

Mitropoulos was a monastic type. He read a great deal, was a scholar, and a highly cultivated man in many areas. He had a good opera background in Europe and, memory apart, was a first-class musician. He knew exactly what he was doing. No one could get away with "doodling" other parts. He would have noticed that in one second.

He was always a gentleman and would never offend or insult a musician, as so many conductors often did. We had no way of knowing his exact feelings towards a section (winds, strings, etc.), or a particular man, but he seemed pleased with us and constantly thanked us for our cooperation.

There is no doubt in my mind that he endeared himself to management in many ways, especially at saving money. He never wanted to rehearse unnecessarily. At times he would state, "Gentlemen, you know the opera. There is no sense in rehearsing further. I'll trust your abilities during the performance." We were often dismissed much earlier than anticipated, which pleased us. When it came to repeating an aria that a singer requested be done over again, he would say, "Please. We'll do it with piano or get a pianist to help. There is no need to keep a hundred men to go over this."

One incident I shall never forget concerned the great baritone, Leonard Warren. He was the number one baritone and the management gave him all the new productions. Robert Merrill and Warren shared the same repertoire, but Warren was the senior member. He had joined the Metropolitan Opera at least four or five years before Merrill when he won the Metropolitan Auditions of the Air, and quickly became an international star, recording in Europe as well as in the United States. Unfortunately he had a super-ego and was a very argumentative man. He did not care who was conducting. At that stage of his career he felt his contribution to the opera was much more important than anyone else's.

Of course, this could never happen during Toscanini's era. He would tell any singer who claimed to be a star, "You must remember, my dear friend, that the stars are only in the heavens. You are just a singer." And it would end there. But with Warren, if a similar situation arose, he would try to convince everyone he was a star and the only one in heaven.

He had made his debut in Verdi's "Simon Boccanegra" in a small role, but now he was singing the lead and title role and was world famous. When he came to the dress rehearsal, which was costumed and with a full cast and chorus, he and Maestro Mitropoulos disagreed on tempi, and interpretation; it did not go well. Warren came down to the edge of the stage and complained that Mitropoulos was not cooperating with him. Mitropoulos addressed the singer very politely, and said, "Mr. Warren, if you had attended our piano rehearsals and private rehearsals all of these problems would have been solved and we would have no difficulty."

Warren went back to his position on stage, then again came to the front of the pit and said, "I'm the star here, and you are supposed to follow me!" Mitropoulos did not deign to answer and then one of the violinists let out a "Bronx cheer," a bleating sound made by putting your lips together and blowing air through. In addition, he stuck his tongue out at Warren. Of course, Warren heard it and came to stage front, thought he spotted the culprit, said "You!" then proceeded to attack him verbally. There was absolute silence in the orchestra. Fortunately, just at that point an intermission was called.

We felt Warren was rough and insulting to "our" Maestro. The intermission was supposed to last twenty minutes, but we held a quick meeting and decided not to return to the pit to continue the rehearsal until and unless Warren apologized to Maestro Mitropoulos. A half hour went by, but he was adamant and refused to do so. Three quarters of an hour went by and the clock kept ticking, and it was an hour. Rudolf Bing came down and beseeched us to go back to the orchestra pit. It was very expensive, this extended intermission. By now we had our union officers down to ask whether we could do this. Could we demand an apology? We found we could do this legally, so we continued our protest.

Mitropoulos begged us to go back. "Gentlemen," he said, "I wish you would drop this issue. He didn't offend me. I don't mind it at all; it's nothing unusual." The men paid no attention. It was one of the few times the musicians, without being asked to do so, took the conductor's side. It was unusual as the conductor is usually an adversary. Finally, after another fifteen minutes, we decided to go back as Warren had agreed to apologize to Mitropoulos albeit reluctantly.

When we assembled to start the next act, he sort of smiled and nodded his head as though to say, "I'm sorry," but he did not exactly say it, so it was not a legitimate apology.

Leonard Warren had very high blood pressure and during a performance of "La Forza del Destino" a few weeks later, he dropped dead on stage of a cerebral hemorrhage. In the early 70's, many years after Warren's death on March 4, 1960, I was attending a reception and saw Mrs. Warren sitting alone in a corner of the room. She smiled at me in recognition of a familiar face and I smiled back at her and walked over to greet her. She said, "Don't I know you?" I identified myself as a member of the Metropolitan Opera Orchestra. She rose immediately and walked away. She blamed Warren's death on that incident in the pit and never forgave the orchestra.

The management was willing to let Mitropoulos choose his own repertoire. He selected "Carmen" and "Cavaliera Rusticana" and "Pagliacci." His was a very unusual interpretation of the work, not the usual Italianate interpretation. It was interesting and always "moved." Mitropoulos had a sense of the dramatic that few of the other conductors had. However, it did not please everyone. Some of the backstage conductors, and some of the assistant conductors, and one in particular, Walter Taussig, came to me once — we were friends — and said, "This is the worst interpretation of Cav/Pag I ever heard in my life!" "But Walter," I said, "it moves. It keeps the singers going. He does not allow them to fall asleep on the stage."

I think Mitropoulos really followed the score and many of the conductors of Italian repertoire deferred to the singers and let them hold notes indefinitely. In short, he was probably performing an authentic version of the score. He never upset singers or drove them unnecessarily but kept the music flowing and going as best he could.

There was only one unpleasant incident I can recall in his stay with us, and it was during a rehearsal of "Carmen" on the roof stage of the old Met. Our first flutist was Jimmy Politis, Greek as was Mitropoulos. Politis had terrible personal problems: His family had left him and moved to upstate New York. He was alone and spent most of his free time in bars. Sadly, he was an alcoholic and the Met had sent him away for a cure a number of times. He never came into the pit inebriated, and most of the time he played well. He protected himself when he knew the days he was scheduled to play. He spent hours before practicing and getting in shape, but his playing gradually deteriorated and eventually he was no longer a first-class player.

He was paranoid, as many alcoholics are. I suppose he was also embarrassed in front of another Greek. What else could have caused him to suddenly say to Mitropoulos, "Why are you always picking on me?" Mitropoulos stopped the rehearsal, put his two hands together as though he were saying a prayer and said, "My dear man, there is nothing I have against you. Your playing is beautiful." He expressed himself as though he were saying, "I don't see the reason for your outburst." The whole orchestra froze. We realized that an alcoholic is not predictable and we could expect anything. That was it, however, and the rehearsal continued.

Another incident at the same rehearsal concerned a horn player, David Rattner, who was having domestic problems and, more serious for us, musical problems. It was referred to as "losing your lip." He flubbed notes and you shuddered when you heard the horn "crack." He collapsed that day with a nervous breakdown, and I took him home. A dramatic rehearsal, to say the least.

Mitropoulos was an enthusiastic mountain climber, had never married, ate sparingly, and was always in good health. Nevertheless, he began to show some signs of heart disease. He took a leave of absence to recuperate. One evening he came back to attend a performance — someone else was conducting — and came down to the edge of the orchestra pit to say hello to us with that wonderful smile beaming from one of the most interesting faces I have ever seen. When we saw him at the edge of the pit after the first act not one of us left. We all stayed to greet him. We all loved him.

He finally returned for a few performances, and the following year, 1960, when preparing "Lulu" by Alban Berg in Italy, he collapsed and died. It was a terrible loss for all of us — the orchestra and the musical world.

The Bing Era

The first fifteen or so of my years at the Metropolitan Orchestra are very clear in my memory — the dates, people, events. But those were simple times. By contrast, the Bing Era, which lasted twenty-two years, witnessed a host of rapid-fire, radical changes. Memories seem to tumble over one another.

When Rudolf Bing came to the opera in 1950, there was no money for new productions and many of the singers on the previous roster were carried over; we even used the old scenery.

Opera itself was confined to a limited audience, the so-called 400 who occupied the Golden Horseshoe and contributed most of the money. The public, as interested as its members may have been in opera, could not afford it. Only a few inexpensive seats and reserved standing-room spots were available, and they were always occupied. The opera in the mid-30's was almost always sold out.

You will notice that up until the 60's I speak of "the men" in the orchestra. The reason is simple. There were no women with the exception of one of the two harpists: Amelia Conti. She was first harpist; later on Florence Wightman came in to replace her. The same man, Sodero, remained second harp.

Then in the mid-40's, Janet Putnam joined us. She is married to David Soyer, the cellist of the renowned Guarneri Quartet who is my wife's brother. Janet stayed with us about four years. Later, when audition procedures were changed and all applicants were behind a screen with members chosen strictly on merit, many women won auditions and entered our ranks. Today, they represent about thirty percent of the orchestra membership.

With the advent of radio and recording the public for opera gradually increased. Bing was well aware that he was expected to make changes to promote the opera successfully if he wished to remain. So, his primary interest and concern was to present new productions. This required a great deal of money, and the contributions and other operating funds were spent entirely on the stage. He was concerned with eye appeal.

The employees complained that everything went for looks to improve the stage and that none of the money went to the orchestra, the chorus, ballet or other workers in the house. Bing often told us of a contribution made by Rockefeller or some other wealthy patron who donated the money solely for the stage production. We were by-passed completely. As a result, we had little or no success in achieving any improvements in salaries, benefits, or pensions.

Along with the new productions, Bing brought new staff—his own staff—to help in administration of the house. His assistant was John Gutman, a critic on a London paper. Max Rudolf became a musical advisor on repertoire while Fritz Stiedry organized a new conducting staff. There were also many changes in personnel in the orchestra, the chorus and the ballet.

Bing was intelligent enough to know what he knew and liked and what he did not know, and he engaged people to advise him. As a result, the next twenty-two years were hectic, often stormy. But in all fairness to him as I look back, great strides were made and the opera attracted a large new audience. Today, opera is a major form of entertainment in New York; we have finally caught up to the Europeans. Some might even say we surpassed them, since the Metropolitan Opera is now considered by many to be the leading opera house in the world.

Rudolf Bing introduced some extraordinary singers to the opera audience: Tucker, Merrill, Baccaloni, Callas, Tebaldi, DelMonaco, Corelli, Freni, Bergonzi, Hines, London, to name a few. He also introduced strict rules and regulations, unlike his predecessor Edward Johnson, and he expected them to be followed. Many people thought him unfair, but he was very critical of the behavior and affiliation of singers.

Take the case of Lauritz Melchior, still our most important helden-tenor, who was beginning to make movies and money. He became a star in Hollywood, but Bing was not happy. He disapproved of what he regarded as a cheapening of an opera star's talents. He criticized Melchior severely, but Melchior chose to do what he wished and in 1954 told Bing off, left the opera, and moved to Hollywood where he lived like a lord. In 1955 he starred in a lavish musical production at Jones Beach, "Arabian Nights." He had become even heavier than before, along the lines of a Henry the Eighth.

I was in the orchestra that summer and every time I would greet him and ask, "Mr. Melchior, how do you feel today?" he would answer in his Danish accent, "Ach! My gout. It's bothering me something awful!"

That summer I became friendly with James McCracken who at that time was in the chorus at the Met, and was engaged to understudy Melchior at Jones Beach. He was waiting for Melchior to cancel so that he would have the opportunity to sing the lead. But they don't make them today like they did then. A singer would appear if he had one leg buried in the ground, and do a job. Today, one cough and they cancel. James McCracken would have to wait to become a great opera star, which he did and which he was some years later. Then Helen Traubel began to sing in night clubs. She did a stint at the Copacabana and a few other clubs. Bing told her unless she gave it up, she could not sing the Met any longer. She, too, said, "Who cares?" and went her way. This incident was highly publicized in the media, as Traubel was still in her prime as a singer, was an attractive woman, and sang all the Wagner soprano roles. We no longer had Flagstad, so Traubel was very important to the company.

Bing was very successful at promoting the new singers he brought to the opera. One of the best was Renata Tebaldi, who made her debut as Desdemona in Verdi's "Othello." Then there was Maria Callas, who made her debut in Italy although she was an American singer. She sang in this country in San Francisco and Chicago, and then came to the Met. Unfortunately, she did not stay too many years with us as there was always some dispute between Callas and Bing. They did not get along at all.

Bing favored Richard Tucker, who had come to the Met during Johnson's regime. He set a record for singing more opening night performances than any other tenor. Richard Tucker would tell me, "It takes ten years of study to learn the repertoire, ten years to make a reputation, and another ten years to live off your reputation." Richard Tucker had a run of successful and great years and was still singing beautifully up to the time of his premature demise.

Karl Böhm came to the Metropolitan Opera in the late 50's, early 60's, He and von Karajan were considered the two best conductors in Europe. Böhm had remained in Germany and Austria during Hitler's regime and was one of Hitler's favorites, so when it became known in the United States that Böhm was arriving there was a great deal of opposition.

At that time there were demonstrations and disruptions of performances in Carnegie Hall and the opera houses when foreign performers and conductors appeared, especially those whose connection with the Hitler movement was known. There were also demonstrations against Soviet artists.

Böhm was known to be a Hitler favorite, but his case was handled very well, as he had already guest-conducted the New York Philharmonic and the Chicago Symphony. By the time he came to the Metropolitan Opera the demonstrations were at a minimum.

Everything he conducted won critical approval. He took over the Strauss, Wagner, and Mozart repertoire. Personally, I found his beat difficult to follow. It never seemed precise to me and I thought there was something lacking in his technique. Eventually, I considered blaming it on myself. Perhaps I did not know the repertoire as well as I thought I did. However, I *had* played all of this before with other conductors and everything was always very clear to me.

Every conductor has his own characteristics, and there is no question Böhm had a big public following. He conducted "Don Giovanni" and "The Magic Flute" and "Marriage of Figaro" by Mozart, Strauss' "Electra" and "Der Rosenkavalier." Then in 1966, in our first season at the new house with a superb cast, he conducted the hit of the season, "Die Frau ohne Schatten," by Richard Strauss. We then prepared a new production of Wagner's "Lohengrin," and it was obvious he was very nervous, and very tense. This production was very different from any other we had done and everyone was on edge.

In a big scene in that production of the opera the chorus was perched on tiers and stood absolutely still for almost an hour. The stage scene looked like the inside of a cathedral with a huge vault of Tiffany-like stained glass. The effect was that of an ancient frieze or tapestry. It was very impressive to see, but the people working, especially the chorus, were greatly encumbered. Many of them fainted from standing without moving under the heat of the lights.

During the dress rehearsal, in front of an audience, Böhm was very much annoyed about many things, but particularly the noise on-stage. The stage hands had to move scenery, had to move about, and communicate with each other. In every performance and rehearsal some sounds come from the stage. Some noise also came from the audience. Böhm, paranoid as most conductors are, was sure this was being done just to annoy him.

He stopped the rehearsal by shouting, "Vas ist das? Ein Caffee Haus?" He was very upset. An intermission was called and then came the "biggie" — the loss of his sweater.

He had an old sweater full of holes, and he usually flung it over the first row of the orchestra seats. When he could not find it at intermission, he made a big fuss and declared that if he didn't find the sweater, he wouldn't continue the rehearsal.

The man could well afford to buy one or fifty new sweaters, but he was in an agitated state and made much of the loss. Later, the lady in charge of the insurance department, Selma Lewis, told me they never experienced such commotion about a lost object. They assured him he would be reimbursed, or they would buy him a new sweater. They put in a claim for $25, for this sweater that probably was not worth twenty-five cents, and we later learned that one of the stage hands saw it, thought it was a rag and threw it out.

Then came an incident I was involved in. On the very last page of "Lohengrin" where the swan pulling his boat arrives to take Lohengrin off through the bulrushes, and away to wander the world, the orchestra is playing the final phases of the opera. There was a pencilled-in note on my part that I had never seen before. Apparently it was made at the prior rehearsal. I had missed that rehearsal, so I leaned over to my stand partner, Leonard Grossman, and asked, "Is that a correciton in the part?"

Böhm saw me talking to him — I am sure he could not hear me as the music was very noisy at that point. He stopped the full dress rehearsal, and angrily said, "Vas ist das?" as if to say, "What are you doing?" I answered, "Maestro, I'm inquiring about a correction in the score!" A few minutes later the rehearsal ended.

Bing, George Schick and others in management came down to congratulate Böhm on the wonderful job he had done. It was quite the custom to congratulate the conductor, flatter him and assure him he was going to have a great success. He may have made some comments to them about the disturbances of the audience and the stage hands, and perhaps about me. I was furious! He never should have made a comment, certainly not stop the orchestra. I was trying to contribute my part to the performance, and if there was an error in the music I did not know about, I wanted to know why and which was the correct version. I stormed over to our first violist, John DiJanni, and asked loudly and angrily, "What does he think this is? A concentration camp? You are not permitted to talk to your partner about the music?"

He saw me speaking to DiJanni in a very agitated fashion. He was still surrounded by the "top brass" and he turned to me and said, "Vat are you saying? Vas, Vas?" I went directly to him and said, "Maestro, this is not a Nazi concentration camp. I'm not being guarded by military men. We're just doing a rehearsal. I missed the previous rehearsal and I wanted to correct a note."

He did not believe me, so he asked me for the part, and there was the proof that there was some question about the score.

We all knew his affiliation with the Nazi movement, and I could not resist the wonderful opportunity to expose a bit of it. No one could question my allusion to this, especially Bing or Schick. They were astounded I had the nerve to make a reference to it. Böhm turned pale. When he was convinced my stopping to talk was legitimate, he leaned over to kiss me on the cheek, but I avoided him and moved away.

After this, his manner was as meek as a lamb with the orchestra. I had accomplished something. I had broken through a veneer that he had, and that had been accepted by the management — that the conductor was the boss, right or wrong. This seemed to impress Bing and Schick.

I went to the orchestra room to dress and put my instrument away. I was speaking to John DiJanni and I was still angry. Böhm came into the orchestra room dressed in his winter overcoat, and scarf (but no sweater), looking for me. When he found me he said in effect that I was a very serious and good violist, and he again tried to kiss me. This time I did not move fast enough and he got me. He patted me on the shoulder, shook my hand while holding his hat in the other hand. He said it was all a misunderstanding on his part. He did not apologize; it really was not really necessary.

Of course, I became an instant hero to the orchestra, as Böhm was much more civil in his later appearances with us. Perhaps I had taught him a lesson, though I am inclined to doubt it.

Thomas Schippers arrived at the Metropolitan Opera in the late 50's. He had made a mark for himself conducting the Gian Carlo Menotti operas — especially the long-running hits "The Telephone" and "The Medium." Through the graces of Menotti and Samuel Barber, he was introduced to the Metropolitan staff and Rudolf Bing, and was given an opportunity to guest conduct. The first opera he conducted as I recall was "Don Pasquale" by Donizetti.

Schippers was extremely good-looking. He was very young, in his 20's, over six feet tall, very agile, thin, and very charming. When he started to rehearse the orchestra, we could tell instantly that he knew what he was doing. He had an unusually clear beat with a beautiful twist to it. It was very pleasant to watch him conduct. He went through the opera, a very tricky one, as though he had conducted it for many years.

Some friends of mine were in the audience at a guest dress rehearsal, sitting next to an old retired conductor, who had conducted opera in Toscanini's time, about 1915. The man was in his 90's and he remarked to my friends, "The boy has golden hands, like Toscanini when he was a young man." It was obvious that Thomas Schippers was going to have a great success.

He returned to conduct numerous performances, but Schippers was not a staff conductor. He was invited as a guest conductor and was beginning to conduct many symphony orchestras including the New York Philharmonic as a guest conductor, and his reputation was growing rapidly.

In most cases when a young man starts to make an immediate success the way Schippers did, the aim is to acquire a permanent place with a symphony orchestra. There were even rumors that he might replace Mitropoulos at the New York Philharmonic. Meanwhile his repertoire became much more extensive. He was always in control and gave a good performance of everything he did. He conducted a new production of Mussorgsky's "Boris Godunov" and was the conductor of "La Forza Del Destino" at the performance when Leonard Warren collapsed on stage and died.

Schippers also conducted Wagner's "Die Meistersinger." However, most of us had seen during the rehearsals that he needed a great deal more experience for that, and we anticipated some mishap during the performance in this opera. Sure enough, just as in the case of Fritz Stiedry, who as I mentioned earlier began to "drown" in the performance (in his case because of old age), Schippers' youth and inexperience did him in. We "swam" for about two pages — also during a Saturday matinee and radio broadcast. It was not a pleasant moment.

Around 1968, my daughter, Phoebe, was studying opera stage production at Indiana University. Schippers had already left the house for the season. I wrote him a note on her behalf asking whether he could possibly use her as an assistant stage director in Spoleto. This was Menotti's "baby" in Italy, where he was producing a very successful annual summer festival and Schippers was the musical director. He wrote me that "All the positions have been filled, though I do not doubt that with her background and the exposure she had to opera she would have fitted in, but perhaps next year."

In 1973 when the Metropolitan produced a very successful new production of "Boris Godunov," the critics proclaimed it the best production ever of the opera — August Everding produced, Ming Cho Lee was the stage designer, and John Dexter staged it. My daughter was now a stage director at the Metropolitan and was assigned to this opera. Schippers came to me later and said he wished he could turn the clock back and have had her work with him in Spoleto. He told me she was the most capable, cooperative, and imaginative stage director he had ever worked with, and they developed a close personal relationship.

She went on to become the Executive Stage Director at the Metropolitan Opera. After the "Boris" production Schippers returned for a few more performances and soon found what he was looking for, a permanent appointment as musical director of the Cincinnati Symphony Orchestra. The members of that orchestra were delighted with him as was the public. He was voted "Man of the Year" in Cincinnati, and built the orchestra into a first-rate organization equal to the Big Five.

Unfortunately, his career was short-lived as four or five years after his appointment he became terminally ill and passed away. He left the Cincinnati Symphony a large endowment. His death was a great loss to music and music lovers.

Max Rudolf was brought to the Metropolitan Opera from Europe by Rudolf Bing, who appointed him primary musical director in charge of musical responsibilities, such as dealing with the orchestra and chorus. Bing and Rudolf were friends. Rudolf was also an excellent pianist, accompanist and coach and therefore was well qualified. For the ten years he was with us, Bing relied heavily on him for guidance relating to the musical matters of the house.

Bing could very well determine what he liked or did not like, but he was not a trained musician and turned the musical departments over to Rudolf. There were often occasions when a conductor canceled all his appearances for the season, or became ill for a performance or two, and one of the assistant conductors would take the podium. Max Rudolf was the equal of any assistant conductor on the staff, knew the entire season's repertoire, and often stepped in to conduct. He was very competent; he had even written a text on conducting that was used in all the music schools and colleges.

Rudolf was engaged by the Cincinnati Symphony before Thomas Schippers. Many of the musicians were unhappy with him there for a variety of reasons.

When appointed to symphony positions most conductors wish to leave their own imprint on the orchestras. The first thing they do is attack the older musicians and replace them, if they can possibly get away with it, with younger men. The older experienced musicians can easily detect if the "Emperor has no clothes" and the young new musicians are in awe of the conductor and tolerate more nonsense. Rudolf tried to raid the Metropolitan Opera Orchestra. One of the violinists, Rafael Feinstein, was approached and offered the position of Assistant Concertmaster. He had recently come from Israel to study at Juilliard and had joined the Metropolitan Orchestra. He had a young family and decided against uprooting his family from New York to Cincinnati. He is still an active member of the Met.

As far as Rudolf's behavior with us at the Metropolitan in those days, he was very pleasant and seemed most sympathetic to the orchestra's problems. We addressed him rather than Mr. Bing or Bob Hermann, who was also a non-performer with no musical training. It was Max Rudolf who arranged the meetings with Bing concerning our pleas for more nights off.

Every symphony orchestra had three or four nights off. We had none. We simply had no free time. We would've performed better if we were not so tired, and we truly deserved this consideration.

After listening to our presentation, Bing, a quick-witted and sarcastic man responded by saying, "I suppose, gentlemen, you would like me to mail the pay-checks to you while you sit at home and come in one or two days a week!"

Max Rudolf was sympathetic to the working musician. He did not treat men like they were some sort of slaves, unlike many conductors who acted as absolute dictators — at least he did not at that period. Later we heard stories about him, after he left Cincinnati, whether at the request of management or of his own volition to become head of the opera department at the Curtis Institute in Philadelphia. He also served for a season or two with the Dallas Symphony. They were having some problems and he acted as musical advisor. He eventually came back to the Met for one or two productions, one of them "Don Pasquale."

His attitude was now so different it surprised and shocked us. He made remarks complaining that he never received the recognition he thought he deserved in his younger days when he conducted at the Metropolitan Opera. Things had always gone smoothly then; he never had any ax to grind, and nothing seemed to displease him in a musical sense. But when he returned in the early 80's he was an entirely different person — very arrogant — and he made a stupid speech to us.

"Gentlemen, I am Max Rudolf. I am not the Max Rudolf you knew before, so please pay strict attention. I want perfect behavior as I want a good performance." Well, this was not the way to endear yourself to an orchestra, although it is not the first time we had this experience with a conductor.

The opera he was directing was "Don Pasquale" by Donizetti, the same opera Thomas Schippers had conducted at his debut with us. Rudolf was not the person to conduct an opera like "Don Pasquale," a fast moving opera that required a light touch. It could be very tricky for a man with Rudolf's Germanic background. It needed an Italian conductor, born into this sort of repertoire.

I thought this performance was a disaster. In some instances, the orchestra fell apart, and no matter what he said to us, or requested, our response was as normal as it would have been for any conductor. We felt he did not know what he was doing. I would not be so bold as to say he did not know the opera, but his co-ordination, conducting with his hands and trying to express what was in the score just was not right. He only remained a season or two, as he had other commitments, and had to fly back and forth to his other assignments between performances of his operas at the Met.

Kurt Adler was appointed by Rudolf Bing as chorusmaster. Like all the people in the organization, he had inherited the old staff, among whom were singers he felt had reached retirement age. He therefore replaced quite a number of chorus members.

As in any organization a new member in authority wants to exercise his position to emphasize his own importance. Not surprisingly, then, as Adler's stature at the Met grew so did his desires. Shortly, he did the same thing that other musical directors did — went to Bing and requested that he conduct performances when a conductor was ill or cancelled.

Adler conducted all the literature that had chorus in the score. After all he was familiar with this repertoire and the chorus was on their toes when he conducted as they did not want him to pick on any one of them later. He had a great deal of authority in his own department. He remained at the Metropolitan Opera in this capacity at least fifteen or sixteen years and retired in the early 70's.

Nello Santi came to the Met in 1962. His first opera assignment was Verdi's "The Masked Ball." He is a large man, about six feet one inch or two and weighs a good two hundred pounds. In spite of his bulk you would think he was an athlete because there was nothing about the man that implied any kind of lethargy or slow movement. He ran up to the podium, and once he began to swing his baton, even though it was no faster than it should have been, the movement looked like the swipes of a whip from one side to the other. He seemed to whip the orchestra into a frenzy. Because of the energy expended, the critics assumed the performance was too loud. When you see a conductor use a great deal of physical movement, it is impossible to remain lethargic and sit back in your seat. You do play a little louder and give a little more. However, he never over balanced the singers. Santi was always aware of that.

Santi's first rehearsal with us was memorable. He conducted everything from memory and there was no doubt his memorization was authentic and not faked in any way. This rehearsal was on the roof stage of the old Met and we were all intrigued with this genial man. But his English was the worst. We always had to get Italian-speaking members of the orchestra to interpret his comments to us.

During a very difficult violin passage — perhaps he thought he would impress us — he walked down through the first violin section of the orchestra. When he arrived at the fifth or sixth stand he cupped his hand to his ear as though he were using a horn to listen to each violinist, and to check on each to hear whether he was playing the passage properly.

When he arrived at the stand where Seymour Wachschal was seated, he stood and played right into Santi's ear. When the musicians saw that they broke into laughter. Santi immediately returned to the podium with a big smile on his face. He got the message that was essentially — your place is on the podium — leave the playing to us.

Santi could play almost any instrument and often demonstrated on the oboe to illustrate how he wanted a passage played. Twenty-five years later — I will not go into the details of his career at the opera — in 1987 the orchestra gave a Christmas party. I had retired from the Met but my wife and I were invited and Santi was there. Whenever I saw him he inquired about our former manager and first violist, John DiJanni. Johnny spoke Italian and often acted as a translator. I told him that I saw John on occason when he came to New York from New Mexico where he lived now. He asked me, "Do you still smoke a peepa, and does Johnny smoke too?" I told him no and we exchanged pleasantries about our families.

Santi has an excellent rapport with the orchestra. He is really a charming man. I would number him in the course of my fifty years of experience as one of the finest opera conductors, with an extensive repertoire — all of which he knows from memory. He is welcomed by the orchestra whenever he conducts at the Met, but even now, so many years later, his English is still terrible.

Alberto Erede and Max Rudolf were friends in Europe. Bing invited him to conduct at the Met in the 50's. He was very young then and had a symphonic background. He had conducted very little opera and made the mistake of telling us so. He asked us to pay attention and help him as much as we could. We saw immediately taht he had told us the truth. He did not have much operatic experience, but since he was such a gentleman we always tried to please him and he always thanked us for our cooperation.

We were performing "Pagliacci" and the tenor, I believe it was Tagliavini, was just concluding the big aria of the first act, "Vesti La Giubba." The tenors want all the leeway they can get in this aria as it is very important and the opportunity for a great success. If he is in good voice, he can hold the last notes, stretching out the aria, and also sing very loud. It is the climax of the first act. At this particular performance, a Saturday matinee, the tenor reached the top note and held it forever. Maestro Erede was conducting, had his hands above his head waiting to give the down-beat that would end the first act. Whether his arms were tired, or he did not realize this was a tenor's heaven, he lowered his arms with a violent down-beat to cut off the aria. Not one member of the orchestra cut off when he did. The down-beat was supposed to coincide with the exact ending of the tenor aria. The tenor continued to hold the note. It seemed like an eternity, but we held it with him. Erede wore a little goatee and he stroked it, and lowered his head in embarrassment.

He came to the orchestra room immediately after we left the pit for intermission, and said, "Gentlemen, many, many thanks. You saved my life. Had you followed me, it would have been a disaster."

It was very nice of him. Most conductors would have blamed everything on the orchestra, even though they knew very well it was their own fault. If we followed every conductor every time, there would be many more disasters. We saved many a conductor's skin.

At the beginning of Rudolf Bing's regime, he wanted to make radical changes. He especially wanted to change the atmosphere of the opera from what it had been during the Depression years of the 30's and he was determined to make his regime at the Metropolitan Opera one of the most brilliant periods of the opera's history.

One of his first projects was to conceive an exceptional production of "Die Fledermaus" to be presented for the Christmas holiday season. He gathered the best cast possible, a superb cast: Ljuba Welitsch, Set Svanholm, Richard Tucker, John Brownlee, and Rise Stevens, and engaged prominent people from Broadway — Howard Dietz and Garson Kanin, who also did the English translation for the stage and engaged Fritz Reiner as conductor. However, Reiner jumped the gun and recorded "Die Fledermaus" during the summer of 1950 for another label.

Bing was furious. He was not about to let anyone steal his thunder, and besides there were contractual obligations the Met had to record the opera with Columbia Records and the original cast. He engaged Eugene Ormandy to replace Reiner, and Ormandy arranged his schedule with the Philadelphia Orchestra so that he could take over this production. We were happy about the new arrival as we were all anxious to work with Ormandy because he had such a fine reputation as a symphonic conductor.

It soon became apparent during the rehearsals that things were not working out the way he wished. He was not happy with the "Broadway" crowd, and like most guest conductors who came to the Met he wanted to establish his authority over everything — the chorus, the ballet, stage hands, solo singers and most of all the orchestra. This kind of authority took years of dealing with the company, so everyone involved knew what to expect from each other. Ormandy had no such background, but he wanted to make it very clear that he could handle the Met as well as anyone. He immediately began to tell us stories. He started off by sort of apologizing that he was a symphonic conductor, but had experience only in Europe conducting opera. Basically his life in America was devoted to the symphony, unlike Stokowski who had presented many operas, especially contemporary ones, in Philadelphia. To my knowledge, Ormandy had never been involved in an opera production prior to the time he came to us.

The first thing he said to us was, "Be very careful to watch me like a hawk, because singers have a tendency to sing sharp whenever they sing loud," so he had to make sure we gave him enough support to see that he achieved the proper balance, and "the opposite is true when singers sing pianissimo." We must be careful not to cover the singers; we must watch him.

He said nothing about covering or what to do if the singers sang in tune. To this day, I have not figured out what out of tune singing has to do with balance from the orchestra. The Metropolitan Opera Orchestra has acquired an instinct, a sort of seventh sense to anticipate a singer. We often know before the conductor whether the singer can be heard, or whether the singer is getting slower, faster, etc. The Metropolitan Opera Orchestra has been referred to as "a musical rubber band," for it is so flexible to the needs of the moment.

When Ormandy made these remarks to us we thought them condescending and unnecessary. Who did he think we were? School children? This precipitated a silent feud. Ormandy wanted to maintain the upper hand at all times, and the orchestra acted the way they normally did. If they had to work harder they certainly would, but if the score did not require it, they relaxed a little.

When the second act opened on the grand ballroom scene, on the ball, the great party, we usually played a Strauss waltz. We were all interested in watching the stage to see the new scenery, costumes and staging. This production was to open on New Year's Eve, then have another nineteen performances — twenty in all that season. Ormandy noticed that no one was paying any attention to him. He noticed it more than once during the performance. When he looked in any direction, all eyes were focused on the stage. Even if we had watched him it would have made no difference as we all knew the waltz from memory, and if not, we faked it.

He complained bitterly to the orchestra manager, John Mundy, and Mundy told him he would handle the matter. He did mention to us that the Maestro had complained and that we should pay more attention to the conductor, and so on. Nothing changed. We all watched the stage at this point in the opera — those who could — and those who did not have a clear view would stand up during musical rests to see what was going on.

This was really "Broadway," the first operatic production like this at the Met. I do not recall what the critical reviews for "Fledermaus" were, but Ormandy continued to carp about nobody treating him with proper respect and finally he got on John Mundy's nerves, and Mundy told him to stick to symphonic conducting and let us lead normal lives at the opera.

About the same period we were rehearsing Verdi's "Requiem" with Bruno Walter. Walter was entirely different in character and personality from Ormandy. He was scholarly and tried to be pleasant, soft-spoken. His English, though accented, had a certain poetic delivery. Ormandy was more showman, bombastic, and even when he spoke English, he sounded Hungarian. Ormandy had been sitting in the front row watching the Walter rehearsal, and at the "break" was getting up to leave when John Mundy approached him and said pointedly, "Mr. Ormandy I invite you to stay for the rest of the rehearsal. I think you would find it very interesting. There is a great deal to be learned by watching Bruno Walter." A few of us heard this as well. It was quite a dig.

Actually, Ormandy was very well-behaved with us. He did not shout and rant as we'd heard from members of his own Philadelphia Orchestra. Outside of his demands, which were petty and silly, he was very professional in his behavior. Since he was not a member of the permanent staff he did complain to Max Rudolf about certain individuals, and often wanted an alternate on a first stand to play solos. However, going to management to complain is not unusual for any conductor, even Bruno Walter. This is the only opera Ormandy conducted at the Met. I do not know if it was by mutual agreement or a scheduling problem, but he was not back again.

William Steinberg came to the Metropolitan Opera at Bing's invitation in the 70's. He had been conductor of the Buffalo Symphony and then the Pittsburgh Symphony. The first opera he conducted with us was "Aida." He was very Germanic in his bearing and this was imparted to his musical approach. His beat was a little like Reiner's, but with a little more swing and sway, and he liked to stab the air with the baton like a swordsman. He always seemed to have a stiff neck. At that time his physical problems were concealed from the public, but later we found he had had a stroke and found it difficult to move his head from side to side.

His "Aida" from my point of view was not the kind of interpretation I would enjoy playing day in and day out. The critics were not too kind to him, but he continued with us. I vaguely recall he did a "Walkure" with us, and again it was obvious he knew the score. He had done it many times in Europe, but again the interpretatioon lacked spirit or enthusiasm — necessary attributes that make an opera exciting.

He was a very scholarly pedantic conductor, but not interesting. He was also very sarcastic. Once he stopped the rehearsal and said, "Even though you are an opera orchestra, 'A' is still 440 international pitch and I would like you to tune to it and keep it that way." The fact of the matter is that the Metropolitan Orchestra is as fine as any symphony in the world. Everyone acknowledges that. However, the heat in the orchestra pit can change the pitch while the orchestra is playing.

Steinberg was given another opera to conduct — Samuel Barber's "Vanessa." We had not done this in a number of years. It had been performed previously with Thomas Schippers as conductor. The orchestra was stunned to find that Steinberg got lost constantly and his interpretation was awful! The singers were very disturbed and it was obvious he did not know what he was doing.

Of course, he was a very sick man by then. Two ladies would bring him down to the orchestra pit and he would laboriously mount the podium. His movements had slowed considerably while conducting. I believe he had had a number of strokes that impaired his motion but not his mind. He died some time after this stint at the Met.

Georg Solti's stay at the Met was brief. He came about 1962 and conducted two operas, one of which was a new version — the so-called Dresden version of "Tannhauser," which we had never done before. All the "cuts" were opened and we played all of the Venusberg music. We use this interpretation to this day, and it lengthened the opera considerably.

When we were introduced to him, my impression was that he was a very proud man, very arrogant. He was very businesslike — "Gentlemen, let's go," and he picked up the baton. He did stop to complain, but not so frequently as to disturb the routine of rehearsal. He put on a good show and the critics liked him. We respected him but were not too involved with him as he was a guest, and we knew he was going back to the Chicago Symphony soon.

I must say that contrary to the stories we had heard from his own orchestra members he was very pleasant to us. I recall one instance when there was a huge snowstorm in New York and half the orchestra could not get to the hall for the performance. I was playing at the second stand and my colleagues at first stand could not get into the city. There should have been ten violas, but there were only five or six. I had to play first viola.

Most conductors want what they want regardless of the circumstances. It was their nature to complain about anything and everything. Solti made no comments. He understood that people could not get to work and we went through the entire opera. He did the best he could and did not make a fuss about it. I thought it very commendable. The public would be very surprised at what conductors are apt to do when faced with frustrating situations as most of them are very spoiled.

Solti also performed the Verdi "Requiem" with us. We were rehearsing on the roof stage of the old Met. There were ten to fifteen trumpets to play a call, and he wanted it played so loud it helped deafen anyone who had any hearing problem. His conception of this work lacked the refinement Verdi would have liked, the kind of refined quality that a Bruno Walter would have shown. I suspect Solti was happy to leave the Met and go back to his Chicago Symphony where he was regarded as a deity by the public and a God of Retribution by the orchestra.

Pierre Monteux came to the Metropolitan Opera as a guest conductor late in his long life. I think he was in his 80's. I do not know how energetic he was when he was young, but when he came to us in the 1953-54 season, he acted like a good fat old uncle. He sat on a stool at the podium and made himself very comfortable.

He was assigned to conduct "Carmen" and "Pelleas and Melisande." The score was before him and we ran through both operas without stopping once. He had the experience and a philosophical attitude that if it goes, it goes, and if it does not, it does not.

He was very pleasant, contradicting the stories I had heard about him from musicians in the San Francisco Symphony, where he went after leaving his post with the Boston Symphony Orchestra. One of the musicians in the orchestra at that time wrote an autobiography about his own career with the San Francisco Symphony, David Schneider, and he credits Monteux as one of the first conductors to build that orchestra into a first-class symphony.

But some of the tales were about Monteux's lack of personal interest in the orchestra: that he was uninvolved; that he would do his job and leave for Europe. He never helped the personnel achieve any of the benefits that were desperately needed by the musicians.

In our case, he was a guest, and was as kind and sweet as could be. Anyone who spoke French was his friend and, of course, there were many in the orchestra who spoke French very well. At the break they would surround him to chat and ask questions. Some of the musicians were his old friends, such as Yves Chardon, who was a cellist in the Boston Symphony in 1917.

Musicians always admired certain things about some of the conductors and were curious about others. I was very young at that time, and our viola section was particularly mystified by his dark black voluminous mustache. After all, he was in his 80's. One day my stand partner, Godfrey Layefsky, and I were chatting with him about one thing and another. He was always friendly and we could ask him all kinds of personal questions, so I remarked, "Maestro, the men admire your mustache. Pitch black and full, but the rest of your hair is snow-white." We did not get a chance to say anything further. He said, "Oh yes, my mother, when she was 92 still had a head of black hair. I must have inherited this."

The critics were very kind to him, especially for the "Pelleas." They felt he was as much a living authority on the opera as anyone, since he knew Debussy well and had conducted the opera in Debussy's time. They accepted Monteux's interpretation as the most authentic.

Our first encounter with Leonard Bernstein was in 1956 when the "Omnibus" program on live television engaged Leonard Bernstein to do a series of lecture-concerts for them. At this time Bernstein was the permanent conductor of the New York Philharmonic Symphony Orchestra, and the darling of New York. In much the same manner as Walter Damrosch had done a half century earlier, he became an educator of the American public. The Damrosch family introduced Wagner to the American public. Brother Leopold knew Wagner personally, and Brother Walter via radio exposed the American public to all kinds of music.

Bernstein, a true genius, was not only a fine conductor but a fine composer of serious music, musical shows, and an excellent pianist. His role as music educator to the American public is well-documented and at this early stage of his career, his services were sought by everyone.

Our first experience was at the old Met on an "Omnibus" program lecture concerning the development of opera from its early beginnings to the modern approach. We spent many hours rehearsing with him in the pit. He was in the middle of the orchestra and there was a piano there so he could illustrate on the piano, stand up to comment and conduct as necessary. The rear pockets of his trousers were stuffed with all kinds of batteries and wires. It was not like today's little mike on a lapel or collar. The lighting for the show was provided by the Metropolitan Opera stage department.

What Bernstein accomplished in that hour and a half was astonishing. He was well prepared, but everything seemed extemporaneous. He used no notes. It was extraordinary. I know of no other musician able to coordinate a program of this kind.

Of course, his primary duty was still the New York Philharmonic and being the innovator he was, he was always very, very busy. The Metropolitan had tried to secure his services but he was not always available, and as

I explained previously, a guest conductor engaged by the opera had to make time to program his schedule so it would not interfere with his own primary responsibility.

He delayed accepting an opera until the Metropolitan offered him "Falstaff." This seemed to meet with his approval. That was in 1964, one of the last new productions at the old house. I am sure he insisted on certain conditions, such as extra rehearsal time, and overtime if necessary, and private rehearsal with the cast. We had an unusual number of rehearsals for this opera. Usually management would guarantee only a minimum number to most conductors, but in the Bernstein case exceptions were made. He was fastidious during all the rehearsals. He repeated and repeated acts many, many times. The average act in opera is two scenes to each act, lasting about twenty minutes each. At times we rehearsed scenes with stops for corrections as many as four or five times.

One day we had rehearsed a very long time, five or six hours. A union rule stipulated we could not rehearse beyond a certain hour — usually 4 o'clock, since the stage hands needed time to set up the stage for the evening performance. It was approaching the end of rehearsal time and Bernstein demanded an extension beyond 4 o'clock. He argued it out with Bing, and Bing told him it was impossible — the rule could not be broken. Bernstein put it to him simply, "If I can't have this extra half hour or whatever I feel I need, I will not continue with this opera, you will have to get someone else."

This ultimatum produced some kind of agreement and the rehearsal continued. The performance was sensational. As far as I was concerned, I felt I had studied the opera with Bernstein and knew it better than I ever had. I am sure my colleagues agreed. He left nothing undone, and the interpretation was the best I have ever been involved with before or since. We were amazed at these rehearsals as his energy was boundless. He drove himself to the greatest extreme. When he got a break he would be puffing on a cigarette and rumor had it that he was on "uppers and downers" constantly. He coughed most of the time, and they say he would take something to slow him down at night and in the morning to pep him up, and if this was true, it probably gave him this unnatural energy.

Bernstein's next engagement with the Metropolitan was eight or nine years later in 1973. After Goeran Gentile was killed, the schedule was upset as he had already planned the season of 1973 and 74. Bernstein had been engaged previously to do "Carmen." He began working on "Carmen" with the same intensity as he had on "Falstaff." The best cast was made available: James McCracken was the Don Jose, Marilyn Horne the Carmen and

BEHIND THE GOLD CURTAIN

Micaela was the Adriana Maliponte.

In spite of his intensity and high energy level, Bernstein was always nice to work with. Though he kept us on our toes, he had a sense of humor and was always understanding and considerate of the job we were doing. He understood how difficult it was to work with different conductors and casts at night, and the different people at rehearsals every day. There was only one episode of tension in the orchestra during these rehearsals between our first flutist, Jimmy Politis, and our first harpist, Reinhardt Elster. I admired Bernstein's handling of the matter.

In the third act there is a little entr'acte for four or five soloists, harp, woodwind, violin and viola, and some background accompaniment from the rest of the orchestra. The matter of intonation came up. Both flutist and harpist were very sensitive about this. Jimmy was particularly annoyed and put all the blame on the harpist and did not hesitate to say so publicly. The harpist kept saying, "I spent hours tuning the harp with the stroboscope and I could not possibly be out of tune. It's impossible."

Once a harp is tuned it cannot be changed quickly, but a flutist can adjust the pitch at any time. The weather or humidity can alter the pitch, or a person's physical condition can change it, but it can be adjusted instantly. The harpist appealed to his colleagues, and the argument went on and on. Bernstein stood by silently and never made one comment. When the two musicians appealed to Bernstein to tell them which one was playing out of tune, he refused to get involved in the quarrel.

I do not know if this was his way with his own Philharmonic Symphony, but he used perfect psychology in this case. It all calmed down, and we proceeded. Neither of these musicians had any great love for one another after that, but they were fussy about this because the performance was to be recorded and everyone wanted to be at his best. It was a very important recording as Deutche Grammaphon had taken over the recording contract. We had many recording sessions, at least ten at Manhattan center for this opera with the cast.

To complicate matters, the chorus went on strike. Chorus members wanted parity — equal pay and benefits with the orchestra. The house objected strenuously as no make-up or costuming was required, and no special rehearsal, but the chorus decided this was a perfect opportunity to make a move. They failed. The management did not agree to their demands and had an outside chorus engaged to do the recording. I do not think they did nearly as well as our own chorus would have, but the recording was finished successfully. After five or six performances at the house Bernstein conducted himself, the "Carmen" was taken over by other conductors.

The next year Bernstein was engaged to conduct the then-new Zefferelli production of "Cavalierra Rusticana" and "Pagliacci." At rehearsal Bernstein told us he had never conducted these operas, but that he had listened to Mascagni's interpretation of the opera on a recording made in the early 1900's. He told us he was going to interpret the opera the way Mascagni did. His main concern was tempi. When we rehearsed with him many musicians felt his interpretation was so slow that Mascagni certainly would not have agreed. I never heard the original Mascagni recording, but the opera moved much too slowly, and the critics and public did not treat Bernstein kindly. After that we did no operas with him, just a few concert appearances. He was a guest conductor at a benefit concert for the company during the long strike of 1969-70 and the last time I performed with him was at a Richard Tucker Foundation benefit where the Metropolitan Orchestra played and he conducted scenes from "Götterdammerung" with Hildegarde Behrens.

In my opinion he was certainly one of the most gifted conductors I ever performed with. Despite the criticism of the press that "he resembled a ballet dancer" and that he had these bursts of energy that found him jumping up and down on the podium, I always felt he enhanced the performance, and his enthusiasm always helped the production. The one exception as I mentioned was the "Cavalleria Rusticana." It was more like a funeral march, and he had no occasion to jump at all. If musicians know the conductor knows what he is doing, whatever movements are used are not apt to disturb them.

During the last concert I performed with him, I remembered all the famous conductors with whom I had performed the Wagner literature, and wished I had had the opportunity to play more of this music with Bernstein conducting as his approach was so exciting — hair-raising, but exciting.

Leopold Stokowski was invited to conduct Puccini's "Turandot" in the season of 1962. The opera had not been performed at the Metropolitan Opera for many years. As a matter of fact, I cannot recall having played it before.

This stage of Stokowski's life — his marriage and divorce from Gloria Vanderbilt — had been well publicized. He was close to eighty at the time and was "horsing" around with his two sons from that marriage, as a father with young sons is apt to do, fell and broke his hip and was hospitalized for some time. As a result he could not attend the preparatory rehearsals with us for the opera.

These often took place three or four months in advance of the regular rehearsals with orchestra and chorus. Sometimes these rehearsals were even held the season prior to actual performance. The Metropolitan Opera sent an assistant conductor, Victor Trucko, to his hospital bed to inform him of progress in the preparation. When he came to rehearsal after his injury, still limping, we learned about each other.

We were not accustomed to any conductor at the opera who did not use a baton. It makes it difficult because of the stage. He was renowned for that batonless technique and, according to the results, many people testify that on recordings he made, no one would know if he used his arms, legs or nose; the results were the best available anywhere and the control of the orchestra, the dynamics, everything was absolutely perfect.

However, we soon found we had problems with his conducting, and he had to assert himself the way most guest conductors do when they come to the Met, trying to impress us that they are "the boss." They always try to show, for example, that they know the opera better than anyone else. Stokowski's approach was one of dynamics. Being an experienced conductor of opera, he knew a great deal more about singers than Ormandy. When Stokowski felt a passage demanded more than the singer could attain, or fortissimo passages that were too much for the voices, he made concessions. He voluntarily reduced the orchestra — he called it "Orchestre de camera" — and he reduced the number of players in those passages. For instance only two violas would play instead of six and the same for other sections. In this way he got the effect he wanted and it made it easier for the singers.

During one incident, he asked us to play softer, more pianissimo, in a certain passage. We played a legitimate pianissimo, but it did not satisfy him. He ranted and raved, "Gentlemen, it must be much quieter!" The second time we reduced our volume and again he stopped and angrily delivered a speech in which there was a rather strange statement. "Gentlemen," he said, "I don't have to do this for a living." He implied that he had plenty of money in the bank and said, "If I can't get what I want, demand, I just won't conduct the opera. We will say good-bye." It was not as polite as that, but it was a very agitated dramatic moment, and we sat there not knowing what to do. No one dared speak to him.

He strode off the podium, walked towards the rear of the auditorium to cool down and came back. We had decided without discussing it amongst ourselves, unanimously decided, what we were going to do on the next request. When he raised his arms and gave us the downbeat, we pretended to play. We put up our instruments but no one played. He said, "That's what I want, gentlemen." I am not certain to this day whether he thought he heard us or not, but no one played a note. He was satisfied and we continued the rehearsal. He had a low boiling point, and was a man who did not change much over the years. He impressed everyone that he must serve music in his own way, and insisted that only his way was the best way.

My next encounter with him was when a reduced Metropolitan Opera Orchestra was engaged for two consecutive years to play concerts at St. Patrick's Cathedral. This was the first time a concert of this kind was presented in the cathedral. Our organist, John Grande, was the man who arranged it all. This was approximately ten years after the "Turandot" and Stokowski was well on in years, probably close to ninety. Conducting in this huge cathedral where the sound reverberated and where it was difficult to hear, he often got lost. Once he could not hear the music or it escaped him.

We could not hear each other, and finally Ray Gneiwick, our concertmaster, stood up behind Stokowski and conducted until we all came together. Shortly after that Stokowski retired and spent the rest of his life in England. He was then ninety-five years of age.

There have been many instances where the concertmaster has come to the rescue of a conductor for one reason or another. One instance was an organist who was Lily Pons' personal coach. He taught her the repertoire for which she became famous at the Met. He was a very polite gentleman and had taken over one performance in the 50's. He conducted the overture and slumped to his knees. We could see he was having some sort of attack. No one volunteered to take over.

This was when Felix Eyle was our concertmaster. Lester Solomon, a horn player, forced the principal second violinist, Walter Hagen, onto the podium. He took over and did a remarkable job. Kurt Adler was then brought in to finish the opera.

Hagen became famous overnight. Frances Robinson, the Metropolitan Opera publicist and great raconteur, made sure that all the proper people necessary to publicize the story were brought in to hear it. Within a day or two Hagen retired from the Met and took over as conductor of the Ballet Theatre Orchestra. He remained with them about ten years, at which point he went into the far nowhere. When we heard about him later, we found he had become a bow-maker in upstate New York.

Zubin Mehta came to the Metropolitan just after the new house opened in 1966-67. He was then the permanent conductor of the Los Angeles Philharmonic and a very young man — still in his 30's. He did not have a great deal of experience at that time as an operatic conductor except for some opera conducting in Europe. He did have a lot of training. He was a former bassist and came from India to study conducting in Vienna.

He told me himself he loved opera — he often attended opera at the Met — and that as a student in Europe he sat in the balcony many times in Vienna and everywhere else he could go, to listen and observe, to absorb as much as he could. When he came to the Met, most of us liked his temperament and pleasant disposition. He was down to earth, very friendly to all the orchestra members. We heard that his own orchestra members called him "Zubie baby" and I know he never objected to being called by his first name. In those days he was a very democratic man and friendly with every member of our orchestra.

The first opera he conducted with us was "Aida." He knew the opera thoroughly although he did use the score. He conducted somewhat like Bernstein in that he had a way of projecting his baton line, thrusting it into the air instead of the conservative usual Germanic way of working in a pattern. Many conductors such as Schippers and Bernstein practically danced around on the podium. He was that kind of conductor. He kept the show and himself moving. I thought the production a success as his love of opera helped to make it successful.

He later conducted an opera commissioned by the Metropolitan Opera, "Mourning Becomes Electra" by Marvin David Levy. I thought it was a very good opera and a very good production, but it was taken out of the repertory because of poor critical reception. Mehta conducted it very well over its run of two years.

Friction between Birgit Nilsson and Mehta regarding a miscue, but I can only discuss this from hearsay. I played the performance but do not remember the details. In any case, there was quite a to-do, and it was not a happy union between them.

Mehta also conducted the last production of "Il Trovatore," which the Met finally dropped in 1988. For some reason the Metropolitan has had bad luck with new productions of "Trovatore." Mehta, as I said before, was a democratic sort and he entertained the "supers" — the spear carriers, or soldiers, or any other characters needed to fill the stage in large crowd scenes. In this case they really did carry spears. In this production of "Trovatore" soldiers were needed to carry spears at the rear of the stage to convey the impression of a huge standing army. Every time there was a pause, Mehta would look up and smile and gesture to imply they should be happy to be holding these huge spears. Every time we saw this, we burst into laughter. This turned that sad opera "Trovatore" into a happy event for us. I hope Mehta will return to conduct at the Metropolitan again.

When I joined the Metropolitan Opera in 1936 Fausto Cleva was already there as chorusmaster in charge of Italian repertoire. He was very efficient and knew the operas very well. Cleva had studied with Toscanini and was very proud of it and often told the members of the company that Toscanini was his mentor. His ambition was to follow in Toscanini's footsteps but history and conditions do not always repeat themselves and he left the Met after a dispute with management. I lost track of him then, but when Fritz Stiedry came to the Metropolitan Opera at Rudolf Bing's request, he was given the authority to appoint and recommend conductors, and Fausto Cleva was one of his recommendations.

Cleva had been an important conductor of the Chicago Lyric Opera and when he needed a conductor there for the German repertoire he had engaged Fritz Stiedry. Stiedry returned the favor by recommending him to Bing and he joined the roster. However, he was not one of Bing's personal choices and although Cleva thought he would be in charge of the entire Italian repertoire he was given standard Italian repertoire to conduct.

Bing himself was also appointing conductors and there was a great deal of competition. We all knew Cleva and liked him very much. He seemed like one of the family. He had two lovely daughters, the elder was at rehearsals almost constantly, keeping him calm. She became a fine singer with the New York City Opera and the younger daughter married one of the fine young men in administration at the Met, Charles Reicker.

His daughter was always present, sometimes both were — to hand him a towel or a thermos of coffee during intermission. He was a slightly built man and quite gentle except when he had the baton in his hand. It was a Dr. Jekyll Mr. Hyde scene and typical of many conductors. He would become tyrannical, impatient, and would blame the orchestra for anything that did not go his way. One of his "shtick" that we disliked was the following: after we had gone through an entire act and got it down to perfection, there was a sigh of relief and we expected to go on with the rehearsal in the hope it would be shortened and we could get home for dinner and prepare for the evening performance. He would inevitably make the remark "Da Capo, Gentlemen," which means "From the top" or return to the beginning, in our case a whole act of the opera. A great sigh of despair and groans arose and another half hour or three quarters was added to the three to four hours we had already put in. Again a "Boheme," again a "Pagliacci."

There was intense competition between the Italian repertoire conductors. The rapport was poor and each criticized the other's work. Cleva was a very talented conductor. He had one advantage that many conductors do not have. He had a thorough training with the chorus and in many, many operas the choral part of the opera is an important, if not as important as the orchestra part. Operas like "Boris Godunov," "La Gioconda," even in "Il Trovatore" the chorus is on the stage practically throughout the opera. The first-rate opera conductor is one who knows every bit of the opera, not just the orchestral part or the melodic line. The conductor must know immediately and exactly the balance between the orchestra and chorus, with the singers, etc.

The criticism I have of Cleva was that he allowed his temper to get the best of him. Instead of remaining calm he would get excited and flustered, and the results were not as good as they should have been from a man of his talent. He did a considerable amount of scolding. He did not have an axe to grind personally, he just wanted to serve the composer's wishes as best he could, but when he was upset the opera, either in performance or rehearsal, did not flow easily. I have found generally that the best results were obtained when everyone was calm and allowed to do his job.

Cleva was also very critical of the interpretations of other conductors. I often heard him speak critically, although it was a sincere point of view, not jealousy. There is no question that he was one of the most qualified conductors during my tenure at the Met. I repeat, every conductor has some shortcomings and his was his temper. It did him a great deal of harm. Had he stayed a few more years and been given the gift of a longer life, he may very well have developed as the most outstanding conductor of the Italian repertoire since Toscanini. He continued to share the major part of the Italian repertoire at the Met until his unfortunate death while guest conducting in Athens.

Herbert von Karajan came to the Metropolitan Opera in 1967. We had engaged Eastern Airlines as our carrier for the opera tours a year or so earlier, and Eastern decided to use its association with us as a great public relations opportunity and offered to underwrite a new production of the Wagner "Ring" cycle. Von Karajan was engaged not only as conductor but as overseer of the entire project. He had a worldwide reputation and many critics and musicians acclaimed him as the greatest living conductor since Toscanini.

Obviously he had vast experience and had conducted in Vienna, Salzburg, Bayreuth, and the Berlin Philharmonic. There was only one drawback — he had been a Nazi and Hitler's favorite conductor. When the Germans came into France, entered Paris, and occupied the country, one of the first artistic events was von Karajan conducting in Paris. Also during the early part of the war he came to the Amsterdam Concertgebow to do a number of performances and recording. They were released in August of 1988. I am sure that in those days, he felt like one of Hitler's sons, and probably wielded more authority than he would have dared in any other circumstance.

The problem for management was how to bring him to the Met. The management knew what to expect — boycotts, demonstrations, as he was one of the two or three musicians who were known collaborators during the Nazi regime. But by 1967 people had swallowed a lot of their resentment and shoved it to the background.

The first opera he chose to mount was "Die Walkure," which is the third opera in the "Ring," preceded by "Siegfried" and followed by "Götterdammerung." When Karajan took over the first rehearsal it was immediately apparent that he had enormous experience. There was no question that he knew the score and that he was a superb conductor. What impressed me more was that of all the conductors including Bodanzky, who interpreted the music and knew the traditional interpretations of the Wagner operas, only von Karajan spent hours trying to make the orchestra sound like a chamber group. I had never heard this kind of effect in "Die Walkure" with the orchestra subdued rather than the other way around. My personal impression was that it had a beautiful effect. It was not necessary to have a blasting orchestra and have singers straining to top the orchestra. I think this approach and interpretation is the most interesting and appropriate way of doing "Die Walkure."

Then came the rehearsals in the pit. What amazed me again was that not only did he handle the orchestra, but he took hold of the stage as though he was pulling strings and pushing buttons on a computer. He had an aide close to him between the concertmaster and his own station on the podium to whom he constantly gave orders, and he kept in telephone contact with the stage to direct every stage direction that took place.

Despite criticism pro and con, he had done his own production in Europe and was well-known as an expert stage director as well as a conductor. Before he came here, the Metropolitan sent a crew of seven or eight to see his production of the "Ring." I do not know if it was in Vienna or Bayreuth, but they all came back with the same comment. "It was a wasted trip because the stage was so poorly lit, so dark, we could not see anything anyway." The lighting choice was his and he intended to use the same technique at the Metropolitan Opera. He did succeed in doing that in New York as this was the effect he wanted.

I had never worked with a man who had all his faculties so perfectly coordinated. He never used a score. He knew everything and was able to direct the stage without the orchestra getting in his way. He put the opera together the way a chess player would finish a game against his opponent in ten minutes. Von Karajan was very pleased with the results he got and his reviews were excellent.

The honeymoon lasted two years. Then he and Bing began to feud. The nature of one of the problems involved rehearsals. He wanted a lot of rehearsals and complained about the orchestra. He wanted additions and changes. The next opera on his schedule was "Siegfried" to be given the following season. He conducted a few rehearsals at the end of the season, and again he was not very happy.

This is a very typical situation with prima donna conductors. They want what they want and they do not understand that the opera is a repertory company and you cannot just do anything you please. It is entirely different when you are leading a group of three or four hundred people involved in an opera production, or a group of one hundred in a symphony orchestra. It is very easy to have a symphony comply with your wishes, especially when you have the authority to order it. However, Bing was still the boss and he had the authority and power, and the financial responsibility to the board, the box-holders, and the public, and he was not about to let any one individual as in the case of Callas, for instance, or a Karajan, tell him what to do.

Although I would have loved to perform the entire "Ring" with von Karajan, that opportunity never presented itself and he never came back to the Met. His career since then is well known, as he always wanted to be an absolute ruler. There were incidents with musicians, with management in Vienna and finally in Berlin where he stood head to toe and insisted on certain conditions; they were not granted and his long association there ended pleasantly.

When the Metropolitan Opera lengthened the season and improved our benefits, its administrators decided to start a summer season at the Lewisohn Stadium, the property of City College uptown at 138th and Convent Avenue. After all, the management did not wish to pay us to do nothing.

The stadium was the former summer season home of the New York Philharmonic Symphony, but they had abandoned it because their extended contract was used to tour. Travel is relatively simple for an orchestra of a hundred compared to the Met, where one had to move three hundred fifty to four hundred people plus scenery, and stage hands, and more.

In any case we began a Lewisohn Stadium season of five performances per week. We did not perform whole operas in concert form but played varied programs with Metropolitan soloists. We also had guest conductors like Arthur Fiedler and a great variety of artists such as Benny Goodman, Count Basie, Ella Fitzgerald and Victor Borge. And the audiences loved it.

One of our guests was Van Cliburn right after his triumphant return from what was then the Soviet Union. He was in great demand and favored us with an evening of three concertos. The admission charges were minimal — from $1 to $3, and there were refreshments available. This was in 1964;

it ran through 1969. Then one summer we exchanged places for one week with the Newport Jazz Festival. We went to Newport and the Newport Festival used the stadium. All this was the result of the contract extension. Management decided to use the personnel, rather than just pay us a salary.

In 1971-72 we had a festival season, after the regular season end in which we performed two or three weeks of some of the most popular operas. That was the period in which a very young James Levine made his debut as the conductor of "Tosca" — the beginning of his brilliant conducting career.

After that we started the park concerts. Since the income was nil, we needed help and had to find sponsors to subsidize the performances such as banks, beverage firms, and the city. This continued in later years, the great difference being that playing in Lewisohn Stadium was only for Manhattan, but today we go to all the boroughs of the City of New York. The stage was donated by Mrs. Guggenheim and when we finished our three-week stint, the New York Philharmonic took over. In these concerts, we gave full-length operas in concert form, usually two operas each summer.

This is the era of the jet age and the best artists are booked years in advance, but management does the best it can. There are also outdoor productions in Europe, so that many artists are unavailable in the summer season. Usually, the opening night of the summer season has a star singer such as Domingo or Freni, and also a star conductor, then these artists usually leave for important engagements in other parts of the world. This gives our staff conductors and younger singers a chance to perform and advance.

The summer activity so beneficial to the City of New York came about as a direct result of the lengthened musician's contract, fought for by the orchestra and finally attained in the 60's.

The roster today is almost entirely from American sources, both singers and orchestra alike. Musical education in the United States has advanced to its present position, the best in the world. Most good universities have a fine music staff and many have artist-in-residence string quartets, and singers, many of whom are from the Metropolitan Opera.

In 1930, there were only two or three first-class music conservatories in the United States, Curtis Institute and the Juilliard Graduate School. Today there is Indiana University, Northwestern, Oberlin — a long and prestigious list. Our singers and players have had the advantage of this excellent training and the audition procedures have changed to the betterment of the orchestra.

In my time an audition consisted of playing some solo work, to show

how accomplished you were, and the rest of the audition was sight-reading. You had no inkling of what music would be placed before you, and you played it as well as you could at sight. You were seen by the conductors and the manager, and there is no question that favoritism was practiced. Today, after qualifications have been approved, applicants are offered the opportunity to audition, and are given a repertoire to learn. They have time to prepare it. They play behind a screen — not only for the conductors but for a committee of orchestra members. There are eliminations from the preliminary auditions to the finals.

This was the beginning of the influx of female musicians, as they are as qualified if not more qualified than many males. This way of choosing personnel has greatly improved the orchestra as entry is based strictly on qualification.

Interest in music and opera had been growing in the United States and as opera companies and symphony orchestras formed all over the country, the need for accomplished musicians was there. In the first third of the century the orchestra was made up of Europeans and then American men entered the orchestra. Then in the 60's women entered our ranks, and today we have a great influx of talented Asians. Formerly most fine black musicians studied jazz as there was no possibility for employment in the classical organizations. This was outright discrimination. Today, however, the black musician of classical training is now entering fine musical organizations. All of these changes began in the late 60's as the contracts for musicians improved, and the orchestras improved along with them. Today, the Metropolitan Opera is an amalgam of all nations.

Epilogue

The preceding stories and reminiscences reveal David Berkowitz's love for the opera and his concern for the individual and collective welfare of his colleagues. He was active all his life in helping to initiate many of the benefits that all symphony and opera orchestras take very much for granted today — the medical insurance, for example, instrument insurance, tax-deferred savings plans, retirement pensions, and even the first American Guild of Musical Artists benefit contract for chorus and dancers was instituted by him.

David realized early on that these benefits were necessary to provide musicians with a modicum of financial security in a very insecure profession. The Metropolitan Opera Orchestra was always the leader. It paved the way for all the other symphony orchestras in the country.

The 1980 contract so ably negotiated by the cooperation of the orchestra committee, attorney Philip Sipser and Joseph Volpe of management was a turnaround in the relations between orchestra and management. Every contract since then has been amicably negotiated. There is comfort for orchestra and management in the continuity of these arrangements. It is a far cry from the Bing era, when musicians were denigrated and insulted by management, creating a hostile, adversary attitude and atmosphere.

The contract in recent years that specified a four-performance week delighted David. It gives the opera orchestra musician an opportunity for normal family living, a privilege earlier members of the orchestra did not have in view of the cruelly all-consuming schedule of the opera season.

"No one can play the schedule this orchestra played before and be a first-class musician. I don't care who you are. You are just too tired," said Richard Nass, who plays the English horn and has been a member of the orchestra for forty-one years. "One of the reasons you have a wonderful orchestra now is that you have a comparatively well-rested orchestra."

Said Herbert Wekselblatt, who has played tuba with the orchestra for thirty-one years: "When operas start at 6 o'clock or 6:30 and ends at midnight, four performances are really the maximum of what we can do, or should do, and that's why the orchestra worked so hard to get a four-performance contract."

Mel Broiles, who was appointed principal trumpet in 1958, observed: "When I started, and for most of David's career, we were liable for seven shows. In the old house, the schedule had us doing seven plus the rehearsals on the roof-stage. The main theme of our labor dispute in 1980 was that we worked even harder at Lincoln Center, and we wanted to have a better life style. Now, I am able to enjoy a little more free time, and take care of all the other things in life that are in many cases a big priority. The players today are walking into benefits it cost us dearly to achieve."

As Mr. Nass pointed out, "We went on strike; we were locked out to have this kind of contract. It is just us old-timers who stuck our necks out and were vilified by the press, management and the public because we wanted a better quality life."

"Having more time to do all kinds of things — go to concerts, practice, reflect, 'chill out' — it has been very, very important. I think it was the turning point, 1980, the turning point in our lives as an orchestra," said Toni Rapport, assistant principal second violin section, who has been with the orchestra twenty-four years. "The contract and the ambiance are so wonderful, they attract better and better people; the level keeps going up."

As a result of the new contract, according to Richard Horowitz, principal timpanist who has been an orchestra member since 1946, "The players are friendlier than they used to be. For instance, the party at Christmas and Chanukah — a lot of people gave of their time and effort. Years ago, we couldn't get a group together to do something like that. The hours were so terrible, we just didn't have the time or energy."

"The orchestra can relax a bit, get some breathing space, so morale is up," said the concertmaster, Raymond Gneiwek.

Gerald Kagan, assistant principal cellist, agreed, adding: "The 1980 contract eliminated most of the internecine strife in the orchestra, and that has made our lives more enjoyable."

The institution of this four-performance contract created the necessity for a large substitute group — essentially a "swing" orchestra to play the three performances not played by the regular orchestra members. At one time, these "subs" were recommended by the Personnel Manager, or a conductor, and they were used whenever they were needed to augment the

Epilogue 169

orchestra for operas with heavy orchestration—i.e. Wagner or Strauss. The members of the regular orchestra agree wholeheartedly that these substitute players should be of the highest quality. Previously, favoritism allowed some unqualified players to "sub," a fact much resented by the regulars, especially since the substitute players enjoy practically the same hard-won fringe benefits as the regular members. Today, they are auditioned, not as strictly as the regular members, but the auditions guarantee that their qualifications are up to the standard of this orchestra.

The large substitute group has changed the inter-relationships within the orchestra. In earlier years, a player sat next to the same person for many, many years. Every member of the orchestra played every performance and every rehearsal, and on the long spring tours, when members traveled on trains together, they had time to spend with each other, and this was a binding influence. Today, if a player has three consecutive days off back-to-back, and another has the same, a musician may not see a colleague for a week or more.

"Having the same player next to you for twenty or thirty years, you learn to work together, breathe together. You know exactly how each of you do things. However, I admit the performances today are better as you are fresher, so you perform at a higher level," said Mr. Wekselblatt.

The consensus within the orchestra is that it is much better today. The continuity of direction by Maestro James Levine has been the greatest single factor in its steady improvement. Mr. Levine has given the orchestra a personality of its own, and the generally held opinion by orchestra members is that he is a most agreeable "boss." The general atmosphere within the company, the ambiance, is extraordinary.

"James Levine is so positive. He never says a negative word. If it's not good, then 'it can be better.' But it's never bad," said Raymond Gneiwek, concertmaster. "Since Mr. Levine came in 1971, his focus has been on the orchestra. Little by little, he has been pulling it up to a world-class symphony. By 'Jimmy' respecting the orchestra as a playing unit, he has lifted its members' self-esteem. The orchestra feels more important, therefore we play better. Whereas back in the '50s, we had to fight to have our artistry recognized and respected. We were treated like a so-called 'pit orchestra.'

"The working conditions are very good now. I've never seen them this way. And as the working conditions have gotten better, and we are going into more specialized things like symphonic concerts and symphonic recording, the morale we have is working to our advantage. There is a nice inter-play with each other and about what we are doing."

Michael Ouzounian, principal violist, insists: "The ambiance here is entirely due to Jimmy. Not only his direction and working with the orchestra, but his whole effect on the place. The way people work here, the way they feel about their work. Also, the feeling of stability. Since the signing of the 1980 contract, it takes that whole stressful aspect out. You really feel secure. I love being with these people, and you know the difference that makes in your life. This *is* your life. You spend more time at the Met than you do at home."

"I don't think the personnel is necessarily better today. We are talking about a very high level of excellent players," said Mr. Wekselblatt. "The orchestra plays better because we have a higher standard, and that standard is that of one musician, James Levine. It's amazing, but in this orchestra there are no 'cliques,' or groups, or anything like that — what I hear about other symphony orchestras. It just doesn't exist at the Metropolitan Opera Orchestra."

"We attract better players because of the higher income, and the better the orchestra, the more fine players who want to play in it," said Mr. Kagan.

Leshek Zavistovski believes that "Having the same music director has created a certain profile for the orchestra. I'll use Maestro Levine's words — a vitality — that is the trademark of this orchestra. There is a winning attitude. Let's play our best.

"I think I was very lucky to join because besides the playing, the quality of life is basically very good. The atmosphere between colleagues is never cut-throat. It's friendly and amicable compared to other orchestras where the feeling is: 'I'm great and I am doing you a favor to play here.' Everybody realizes that we work hard, we have long performances, and we do our best and feel friendly to each other. I don't know what contributes to this, maybe just luck, the people, the people who join us are just good people."

"There is a certain close feeling. Compared to the stories I've heard from other orchestras through the years, no one on speaking terms . . . We have coffee breaks together," said Patricia Rogers, principal bassoonist. "There is no feeling of enmity or anything like that. Everybody gets along."

And Toni Rapport added: "The atmosphere in the orchestra is a very positive one. It did not start out that way. Before 1980, there were a lot of complaints, some legitimate, some otherwise, but there was a lot of discontent. I don't think that exists now. The bitterness of the Bing era, that's gone and it makes a huge difference. In general, the atmosphere is an extremely positive one."

David Berkowitz would have been deeply gratified to see "his" orchestra appreciated by the musical community and public alike today — an

Epilogue

appreciation long overdue. He had always insisted that it was the equal of any symphony in the land.

In his reminiscences David frequently commented on the problem an opera orchestra faces vis-a-vis the symphony orchestra. The literature is just as difficult and often the same. The opera orchestra must be a Gemini—able to accompany a myriad number of conductors, singers, chorus, and ballet, yet be able to perform the symphonic repertoire well. After all, festival programs of music by Mozart, Beethoven, Wagner, Strauss, and other composers are announced with great fanfare by symphony orchestras, but the Metropolitan Opera Orchestra performs this music regularly during every opera season.

The next chapter of David's writing agenda, unfortunately never written, was about a period particularly dear to his heart — the era of James Levine as Musical Director, and of his daughter Phebe Berkowitz's affiliation and great success with the Metropolitan Opera as Stage Director, and Executive Stage Director.

Phebe's association with the opera was a great source of pride to David, and gave him the feeling of a continuous personal relationship with the company even after he retired in 1986. He loved to tell the story of the repositioning of his identity. Before Phebe joined the company, she was David Berkowitz's daughter, but after she joined he became known as Phebe Berkowitz's father.

David Berkowitz had many more tales to tell, but became ill with lymphoma in the spring of 1989 and passed away on September 28, 1989. Wherever he is, he is smiling. His love and pride in the Metropolitan Opera Orchestra is now corroborated by all.

— Dolores Soyer

DAVID BERKOWITZ joined the Metropolitan Opera Orchestra as a violist in 1936 and retired in 1986. His fifty years of service was the longest in the history of the Metropolitan Opera Association.

As a tribute to his dedicated service, the Metropolitan Opera Association dedicated a performance of "The Marriage of Figaro" to him. No other instrumentalist has been so honored in the history of the Metropolitan Opera Association. Director James Levine presented him with an inscribed baton used that evening to commemorate the occasion.

Prior to joining the Metropolitan Opera Orchestra Mr. Berkowitz was awarded the New York Philharmonic Scholarship to study with Rene Pollain, and was a member of the Childs (later called the Oxford) String Quartet. During the years 1934 and 1935 they broadcast the first live chamber music concerts on radio in the United States via Station W2XR, known today as Station WQXR. He was partly responsible for helping to improve the working conditions and benefits of musicians at the Met, especially in the area of insurance protection.

Mr. Berkowitz loved the opera and his colleagues, and was pressed by them to write the story of his experiences. The book was written in 1988 and 1989 but was not transcribed from tape until after his demise in 1989. His collaborator and editor, Dolores Soyer, completed the work in 1994.

DOLORES SOYER was born in Philadelphia and pursued her piano studies there with Harry Kaufman and Sylvan Levin of the Curtis Institute of Music.

Her family is well-known in the artistic and musical world of the U.S. via her late cousins, the artists Raphael, Moses, and Issac Soyer, and her brother David, who is the cellist of the famed Guarneri String Quartet. When her family moved to New York City in 1932, she and her brother continued their musical education. Dolores studied with Erno Balogh, the accompanist and coach for Fritz Kreisler and Lotte Lehmann, her brother with Joseph Emonts, as a New York Philharmonic Scholarship student, and then with Diran Alexanian the great pedagogue and cellist.

In the late thirties and early forties Dolores Soyer became the accompanist for the Master Class of Diran Alexanian and pianist for the Katherine Dunham Dance Company and also to many individual artists. From 1947 to 1952 she lived in France and concertized in Western Europe under the management of Natalie Bouchonnet.

After her return to the United States she resumed teaching piano and coaching in New York City and is still an active participant in the musical life of New York as a teacher and accompanist.

DEC 2 3 1997
DEC 3 0 1997

14

HEWLETT-WOODMERE PUBLIC LIBRARY

780.92 Berkowitz
Berkowitz, David
Behind the gold curtain

28 Day Loan

Hewlett-Woodmere Public Library
Hewlett, New York   11557-2336

Business Phone 516-374-1967
Recorded Announcements 516-374-1667